In Search of my Soul

A captivating and inspiring journey through life.

© *Lucy Pignataro, 2012*. Except as provided by the Copyright Act 12/3/2012 no part of this publication may be reproduced, stored in a retrieval system or transmitted in any form or by any means without the prior written permission of the publisher.

All rights reserved. No part of this book may be used or reproduced by any means, graphic, electronic, or mechanical, including photocopying, recording, taping or by any information storage retrieval system without the written permission of the publisher.

This is a work of fiction. All of the characters, names, incidents, organizations and dialogue in this novel are either the products of the author's imagination or are used fictitiously.

Inner Light Publishing books may be ordered through booksellers or by contacting:

Inner Light Publishing
A Division of Adoptamum.com
www.adoptamum.com
innerlightpublishing@gmail.com

Because of the dynamic nature of the Internet, any web addresses or links contained in this book may have changed since publication and may no longer be valid. The views expressed in this work are solely those of the author and do not necessarily reflect the views of the publisher and the publisher hereby disclaims any responsibility for them.

The author of this book does not dispense medical advice or prescribe the use of any technique as a form of treatment for physical, emotional, or medical problems without the advice of a physician, either directly or indirectly. The intent of the author is only to offer information of a general nature to help you in your quest for emotional and spiritual well-being. In the event you use any of the information in this book for yourself, which is your constitutional right, the author and the publisher assume no responsibility for your actions.

ISBN: 978-0-9872818-0-7 (sc)
ISBN: 978-0-9872818-3-8 (e)

*From all negative situations
is the potential for a positive outcome*

Karen Mc Dermott

Preface

This book has come forth from my own spiritual awakening. That has taken me on a journey through life in ways I had never imagined. This journey has taken me to deeper levels of my being.

Exploring and uncovering aspects of myself that were so deeply hidden and in need of expression. It was the constant restlessness that would drive me to search, heal and have faith that all things can be overcome and restored to perfect balance, leaving me with a feeling of contentment and at peace with myself.

I encourage anyone brave enough to take the road less travelled and journey within. To face to their fears and expand the heart to truly know and live from the space of the inner self.

I hope that my book may inspire and encourage you to take your own journey and shine your light in the world you live in.

Acknowledgements

This book would not exist without the encouraging positive support of Karen and Donna, at adoptamum.com, I knew there was something special about this site when I first set eyes on it, little did I know where it would take me.

To my wonderful loving husband who never wavers in his unconditional love and support even when he doesn't completely understand what I'm on about.

To my two beautiful children you inspire me to keep going, to be the best that I can be.
Thank you for your trust and unconditional love.
Know that you are great gift and blessing in my life.

To our trusted friend and talented graphic artist Simon for helping me put the finishing touches to this book, thank you.
Thank you to the clients that have come through my practice, it was through you that I saw a need for this book to be written.

And lastly to all the people past and present who have crossed my path and shared aspects of my life thank you for lessons that came to me through you.

To my creator for without you none of this would be possible.

Sensing Spirit

How will I come to know you?
I am a whisper in the breeze of the wind.
Be still and listen; you will hear me
I am in the flow of a running stream
Be still and listen; you will hear me
I am in the music that captivates your heart
Be still and listen; you will hear me
I am in the breath you take between your tears when your heart is breaking
Be still and listen; you will hear me
How can I feel your presences?
I am in the breeze that caresses your face in a subtle wind
Be still and feel my presence
I am in the wave that washes over your feet when you stand on the oceans shore.
Be still and feel my presence
I am in the hug of your children when they wrap their arms around you
Be still and feel my presence
I am in the sun as it beams down on your being on a bright, sunny day
Be still and feel my presence
How can I speak to you?
Speak to me in the silence of the night before you close your eyes
I promise I will listen to you
Speak to me when you open your eyes first thing in the morning
I promise I will listen to you
Speak to me when you greet your family at the breakfast table
I promise I will listen to you
Speak to me on your way to work and interact with the world
I promise I will listen to you
Speak to me night or day, when you're sad or happy
I promise I will listen to you.

Table of Contents

Chapter 1	*In Search of my Soul*
Chapter 2	*Acceptance*
Chapter 3	*Fear*
Chapter 4	*Anger*
Chapter 5	*Trust*
Chapter 6	*Forgiveness*
Chapter 7	*Giving*
Chapter 8	*Courage*
Chapter 9	*Love*
Chapter 10	*Marriage*
Chapter 11	*Parenting*
Chapter 12	*Our Beautiful Bodies*
Chapter 13	*Money*
Chapter 14	*The Blessing of Life*
Chapter 15	*Meditation*
Chapter 16	*Friendship*
Chapter 17	*Gratitude*
Chapter 18	*I Found my Soul*

CHAPTER 1
In Search of my Soul

At the tender age of 20, my life was changing. I started to feel differently. I can't even explain what this feeling was; maybe it was depression, as it is known these days. Life suddenly felt different. Relationships fell apart, my work and workplace were becoming dull and boring and no longer satisfying; friendships were no longer exciting and just seemed empty. I was finding it harder to be happy and find fulfillment in anything I did. I began questioning myself: what happened to that fun-loving, carefree girl I used to be? I had always been the one who could find humour and joy in just about anything. Life had become so dry and lifeless. I had not long been out of a relationship that was a roller coaster of emotions and mentally abusive, yet I had convinced myself that, after we were married, it would be different. It wasn't long after this break-up that I developed an eating disorder. I questioned whether it was these events that were making me feel like this. Then again, I had experienced other breakups and I had seemed to bounce back!

The days were becoming more and more challenging. Was I missing something? I just felt so empty. I would break down and cry at the drop of a hat; it seemed easier to cry than get angry. The things I felt I could once depend on just didn't seem to help. What once put a smile on my face now made me miserable; things I had never given much thought to suddenly become obsessive. I started to feel like I didn't fit in anywhere; I felt a sense of not belonging to anything. Home didn't feel right and neither did work or friendships, I just couldn't seem to find my place or connection. If ever I felt lost and confused, it was now; and feeling like there was no one I could trust to talk to seemed to make me feel worse; how could I tell anyone what was going on when I couldn't explain it to myself? They would probably think I was going mad and let me say there were times when I thought I was losing my mind.

I woke up one day and felt like I was standing in front of what seemed like unfamiliar territory. It felt as if I was standing on a road that was blanketed with debris, rocks and mountains that was blocking me from seeing what was in front of me. I felt lost and was overwhelmed by the fear of what I saw and felt. How did I get here? How did I lose my way? No one else seemed to be here. I felt like I was standing alone; nothing about this experience seemed familiar. I then started having strange dreams; the best way to describe them would be out-of-body experiences, like I was being propelled through places by this amazing energy and even though it felt strange, I wasn't afraid until

I was back in my bed and I realized what had just happened. How does one explain these things? At this point in my life, I had never heard of out-of-body experiences, let alone had one myself. I felt a strong calling of God! Again, I had never had a God experience or even knew what that was; I just had this strong, strange sense of a God-like presence. It sounds strange and it was a very strange experience. My sense of what I was feeling and experiencing was that God wanted me to be a nun.

All I could think of was: how do I tell my parents? I felt I had thrown enough challenges their way. How do I explain this strange feeling that is going through me? They weren't overly religious; Dad always wanted me to be a lawyer, to get a good education and be something with a title. I was not sure that he would welcome a daughter as a nun with open arms; I don't think he saw me as very holy.

Of the seven siblings, I was the one who kept rocking the boat, the one who would make others sit up and take notice, even when I'm sure they would have preferred to bury their heads in the sand.

Not sure what to make of this experience, I decided to ask others who crossed my path, "Surely this happens to everyone? Doesn't it?" Yet no-one I spoke to seemed to know what I was going on about, that was until I met a lady who seemed to know this territory well. She referred to it as the "path to God." "What does that mean?" I asked. She said, "Walk it and you will find out." She recommended a couple books for me to read. One was "feel the fear and do it anyway." Looking back, I think it was certainly an appropriate book for me to start with. I was not sure what the path to God was or that I really wanted to know. My experience of God was with the nuns in Sunday school and the priest in church at Sunday mass, where it was ingrained in me and everyone else that "If you

sin you will be punished," so I wasn't jumping out of my skin to get to know God or travel his path.

Yet I stood there, because, despite the mess in front of me and the fear that was growing inside of me, there was something familiar beckoning me to take this path. I started by going with the God I was taught about. I began to visit our local parish and just sat there. At times it felt like I sat for an eternity, expecting God to appear before me and make things clear. I tried a few different parishes but God never appeared, there were no signs, no flashing lights, not even a priest or nun in sight to shed some light. Deep down, I was hoping for a vision: for a tangible god to appear and give me directions just like a parent or teacher give a child direction, but it didn't happen. Feeling none the wiser, I stopped going to church and just felt lost, confused and abandoned by God. What now? Where do I begin? What does one do when life takes you to path that is so unfamiliar and it seems there is nowhere else to go and standing still just doesn't work? I broke down and cried something I seemed to do a lot of these days. In my despair, the only thing I could think of doing was to start looking for ways to move forward on this path and I learned very quickly that it pays to be creative. Debris and rocks don't move that easy and mountains are hard to climb.

I'm sure some things were set in stone and it wasn't always easy to identify what all this stuff was made of, so I tried shifting what seemed remotely familiar and easy. At times, dust would fly up and blur my vision, creating frustration.

I soon came to understand that the dust was a lot of resistance and not knowing how to let go. There were moments that would be so overwhelming that I would break down and cry and scream out to God that if this was the path that would lead me to him, why wasn't he here helping me? At other times it seemed the more debris I moved the worse it got, it would propel the stuff at the back forward, making the task just seem impossible, like nothing had been shifted. Then, there were times when the mountains in front of me seemed insurmountable.

They were the most challenging: when the climb was so steep and there seemed to be nothing to hold on to and the fear was crippling and only blind faith to keep me going. I would humour myself by thinking, "if I can just make it to the top I'll be closer to god and then he'll see me and help me." The laugh was on me: God doesn't work that way. Then, when I thought I was getting a grip on my life, "yes, I know what I want:' I was ready for another relationship. It had been a few years since the last one and I was now a little wiser. The wounds had healed, or so I thought. Life has a way of teaching you, if you let it. As fate would have it, I met a wonderful man with whom I felt a strong connection. It felt different than past relationships; there was a gentleness I hadn't seen in other relationships. He seemed to know how to lift me up and strengthen my faith when life challenged me and it seemed I could do the same for him when the he faced his life challenges. Like me, he came with his own story and baggage. I was more than ready to accept his story because I believed it could turn out to be a great blessing in our journey together. Little did I realize, my parents weren't as accepting as I was and again I became the thorn in their side, taking them out of their comfort zone. Marriage to a divorcee was not what they wanted *in* their strict Italian family. My stubborn nature and determination to fight for what I believe in gave me the courage to stand my ground. If, at 27 years of age, I didn't know what I wanted, I was asking for trouble. This just became another mountain to climb and like all the others, the climb wasn't going to be easy. God had a plan, another strong dose of tough love and valuable lessons that need to be learned; however, this time I wasn't alone.

The next couple years made my early twenties pale in comparison. The pain of planning my wedding without the support of my mother or father, then going through the happiest day of my life knowing that my parents were also dealing with a lot of their own personal pain seemed a lot to deal with.

Nevertheless, we got married and I took off on my honeymoon and just forgot about everything and focused only on my husband and myself. This seemed a long time coming and I was not going to let anyone take away the joy and contentment I was feeling. The joy was short-lived: 8 weeks after my wedding, we tragically lost my father to a car accident. It was hard to process when I'd watched my father and mother work so hard to raise a family and when I thought they just might get the chance to enjoy their lives together. Mum lost him. As I struggled to come to terms with the loss, I found out that I was pregnant. I found it difficult to register the pregnancy, since grief has a way of consuming your whole life.

The days became weeks and before long I was in my second trimester. I remember saying to my husband, "I'm ready now to focus on our baby; I barely finished the sentence only to find myself in a doctor's surgery as she tells me the pregnancy needs to be terminated, the term she used was "a bad formation." There's that mountain again, this one just seemed to get higher and higher. I felt like I could barely catch my breath and that I was sliding down that mountain again, feeling like I couldn't take any more. God must have really wanted me to learn a lot really quickly.

He had one hell of a plan we then lost our home. I felt like screaming at God, "Are we done yet?"

This was becoming a bad dream; one I felt I would never wake from. I kept going even when everything in me wanted to run in another direction. Direction? What other direction? There was nowhere else for me to go. I wanted to find another path; one with no rubbish, but it was too late to turn back. It seems once you set foot on this path you can't go back, at least that's how it felt to me. It's about finding the strength and courage within to just keep going no matter what. I would look back and see what I had moved curiosity and a frustrated life gave me the courage to keep going, day after day, rock after rock. At times, I would call on others to assist me; this would help to shift the bigger rocks and learn something new about myself and the path I was on. It seemed to take forever to notice any change, yet after some time I could see the path's surface. It was breath taking! The surface was smooth and clear with a shimmer of gold. "Wow," it was like being on a treasure hunt and striking gold. These moments made me stop and reflect and look around. These moments showed me parts of myself that I hadn't known before and made the work worthwhile. I wanted to stay in these moments forever.

Some days the rocks were so big and so heavy that all the prodding and pushing and screaming did nothing but create more frustration. It was these times that I learned to be still and catch my breath, feel the fear and rest and in time I would build up the strength to move the rocks or climb the next mountain, further revealing a smooth golden surface, another sunrise to inspire me that I was on the right path and that all is as it should be, all the while learning more and more about myself and life. I once read a book called, 'The Game of Life and How to Play It' and I didn't understand a word of it. This journey was now making this book very clear to me. I was learning how to play the game. It was in these moments that I would be so excited and would share with anyone who would listen, (some would, others would just move away.)

The journey on this path was beginning to take shape. It was beginning to reveal that there was more to me than my physical body. The path continued to reveal more and more aspects of myself, not all were great qualities and some I would have preferred not to know, but we all have shades of dark and light that make us so perfect. I was starting to find out that I didn't need to hide myself behind a myriad of masks. I felt like I was being created, only this time I was aware of the person I was becoming and I was beginning to like this person, warts and all. I was learning how important it was for me not only to allow myself to feel my emotions, but to give myself permission to express those feelings. It was becoming more and more apparent that I really struggled with my true feelings and self-expression, hence the eating disorder and food addiction. Addiction is like a very destructive love affair: you know it's bad for you, everything in you knows the pain you'll suffer when the seduction is over, you swear to yourself you'll never go there again, but something in you is so desperate for love and fulfillment that it makes you give in over and over again and allow yourself to be seduced. Addiction of any kind is one of the most painful experiences anyone can go through, but when you are dealing with food that is a necessity for survival, it takes a lot of deep contemplation, discipline and bloody hard work to overcome the addiction.

No matter what life threw at me, or the obstacles that got in my way nothing could deter me from this path. I was determined to find the end. I thought I would find a pot of gold or something. I often recall as a child being told that if we got to the end of a rainbow, we would find a pot of gold. I wasn't really sure that gold was what I wanted, I just wanted to understand life, I wanted to understand me, I wanted something to make sense. I wanted to be happy and know that I would do whatever it takes to find that happiness, or at the very least understand where to find it. It pays to be stubborn on the path to God. I just became more determined to stay focused, even when others thought I was maybe a little crazy. Crazy worked for me. I would become so frustrated when I couldn't move the rocks or climb the insurmountable mountain in front of me that I would scream that God really needed to show up and give me a hand, this really wasn't a job for a girl to do on her own. So many times, I found myself shattered that God didn't think I was worth saving. I would cry out that if there was really a God and he really cared, he would help me, he would reveal himself and perform a miracle to help me out of this pain, after all that was his job to grant miracles! But it just never happened. The way I saw it back then was: God isn't showing up anytime soon, so I may as well keep going.

I wanted a tangible God, one I could see and touch, not one that I could only get a sense of, what sort of God doesn't show himself? That was the other thing I just assumed, God was a male, not that it made a difference. Male or female, I just wanted God to come out of hiding. I guess I needed to see to believe that God really did exist. I started to find different ways to move the debris and rocks, to climb mountains. Sometimes it was physical work; sometimes it was seeking the help of others. It was at this point I was introduced to meditation and I found other people who were on the same path. Through meditation, I started to really understand the art of silence and contemplation, which is not the same as analyzing. It was looking at what was there and reflecting on what I was seeing and other times it was doing absolutely nothing, through meditation I began to learn what surrender was and how to let go. I'm still no expert, but I'm working on it.

This is where I got to know the times when God would take over and give me a rest and when I realized what I had long thought, "This is one hell of a job for a girl to do alone." The further down the road I got, I learned to stress less, I learnt to trust that with patience and faith, the rocks would move, the mountaintop would be reached and the path would reveal itself. I learned that I could slow down and enjoy the journey as it revealed itself and that the path was long and there was no rush to get to the end. This path is never-ending and as long as I draw breath I have time to travel.

This path gave me many wonderful experiences and many not so wonderful experiences. I learned to embrace the wonderful ones like a token for a job well done and to learn valuable lessons from the not so wonderful experiences. I have learned that there are no mistakes in life, no failures, just experiences to teach us how to be the best we can possibly be in any given moment, no matter what is happening. I have learned that we only ever have this moment, here and now. The past can't be erased, but can be used as a tool to do things differently or to heal, so the road ahead may be walked with greater meaning and purpose. I have learned that it is not what happens to us that causes our suffering; rather the story and dialogue we attach to what happened and that it takes a lot of reflection and contemplation to be courageous enough to let go of the story.

I have learned that material things might make me comfortable and might alleviate some stress and at times create a lot of stress, but they don't fulfill me or define me. I have learned that loving another is painful and empty if I can't love and accept myself first. I have learned to be brave enough to look at myself before I point the finger of blame at someone else. I have learned that it is those moments when we really feel so alone and lost and feel we can't go on, when God is holding us very tightly. Only in the stillness and silence will we be able to hear the reassuring words to keep going.

I have learned that different people will need different ways to move the rubbish, climb the mountain and rocks on this path, even when the end result will be the same. I have learned to trust myself from the inside out and when in doubt, be still. God will speak to me and I need to be ready for when he does.

I have learned that not everything that looks bad is bad. It is these times when the greatest lessons reveal themselves.

I feel like every lesson I learn along the way shows me another piece of who I am at the core of my being. This path has taught me not to get caught up in body image because that's not who I am, not to get caught up in my job title because that is not who I am, not to get caught up in my social status, because that is not who I am, not even my role as a wife, mother, daughter, sister, or friend can define me. They are all roles I play in the journey of this life.

What defines me is not my roles, but my ability to stay true to my spirit and honour my truth in the roles that I play. I believe the greatest lesson has been that God is not some little or big man or women sitting in the sky dishing out punishment and praise on those of us who think we have sinned, that I wouldn't find him in my local parish, mosque, temple, or book for that matter. God for me was found right within my being, guiding and supporting me every step of the way: nothing was out of place. God is my spirit, the very essence of who I am, the energy that created me. God was with me the whole time; he never once left, I just had too much rubbish and dialogue going on within me to notice when he was trying to get my attention. Silence and stillness are the keys, faith is the door and trust is what takes us through the door and to remember that the world is a stage on which I get to perform and that a power far greater and more intelligent than anything I can imagine is directing my life. My role is to show up every day and be conscious and aware of what and how I live this life. Everything I need for this journey will be given to me and everything is exactly as it should be. Even as I write this I know I have barely scraped the surface, my journey is far from over and every day brings another opportunity to get to know myself and learn to express that self which is God personified, it has been this amazing and I say amazing (not that I enjoyed the suffering) journey, because of the lessons learned along the way. I now take those lessons into my life as a mother, wife, daughter, sister, friend and work as a therapist and help others find their way. To be given the privilege to share in another's path is a great honour.

I hope through sharing my experiences that others who may be confronted with this same path will find the courage within themselves to take the steps forward, climb those mountains, shift those rocks and clean the crap that's in the way. I can say the road ahead is exciting, inspiring, uplifting and divine.

You can ignore all signposts and the nudges that are a constant in life and live a life of maybe, someday, or if only, or you can stop right now and start to read those signposts, look at what is trying to get your attention and step off that safety net. As someone once said, "you will never know how great you are till you're standing on the edge of destruction." Nor I am suggesting that it will be as painful or as long, not everyone holds on as tightly as I did; and you had better have a good sense of humour, because you are going to need it to laugh at yourself along the way.

I have walked and lived this path consciously now for nearly 30 years and there were a few battle scars and some bruising. If I had ignored the signposts, it might be a very different story, but there most certainly are no regrets.

May your journeys be as fruitful, exciting, enriching and full of wisdom and may it light up your lives as they did mine. While I will never know or really understand the mystery of God and why some unexplainable things happen, the things I do understand have been for my greater good and I hope for the greater good of others.

God bless

Chapter 2
Acceptance

This was the lesson that I can say challenged me the most throughout my journey. Up until I began my spiritual journey, I had never thought about acceptance, what it means, how it impacts my life, or the difference it would make if I paid more attention to the things I willingly accepted and the things I wasn't accepting.

According to the English dictionary, acceptance means "consent to recognize, believe, or agree to."

There were many more definitions, but these are the ones that best resonated with me. The things that challenged me the most were being able to accept the changes that were happening within me, feelings I had never experienced before and at times a sense of doom and darkness. I struggled and resisted what was happening and would just bury myself in my work and pretend nothing was happening. It didn't work. I couldn't keep going and I certainly couldn't keep pretending. I needed to face these internal challenges and accept that something had to change. It was through accepting these changes that all the things about myself that for so long I had never acknowledged started to surface one by one and not always in the same order. I was beginning to see the many masks I wore to cover up the aspects of myself that I felt were unacceptable. I began to recognize that I couldn't accept the feelings that would arise within me from different experiences. I would use cigarettes or food to stuff them down. There were feelings of anger, sadness, hurt, shame, rejection and a lack of self-worth, just to name a few. I wasn't even aware at this point that those visas were being used for the purpose of numbing and suppressing what I was so afraid of feeling. Therefore, whenever I tried to give up the cigarettes or control the food addiction, I would be so overwhelmed by my emotions that I couldn't cope. And, in the beginning, I didn't know that the discomfort and uneasiness I was feeling within myself was because I wasn't allowing myself to feel the emotions and allow them to move through me; I just kept stuffing them down. It was only through continually exploring my spiritual nature and peeling off layer after layer that I was able to begin to acknowledge and accept the good, the bad and the ugly parts of myself and all those emotions. And there was a fair amount of each. It was only when I learned to accept myself, encompassing both my shortcomings and my greatness that I began to heal. After that, it became easier to accept others shortcomings and their greatness. This didn't happen overnight; it took a lot of conscious effort and compassion for myself when I struggled with accepting what was. There were many things in my life that I accepted blindly, like believing that others were smarter or more beautiful than I could ever be. Never did it occur to me to question how I came to that conclusion, or that people with more money or material things than what I had must have been better than me. If people used or abused me, I just accepted that it happens and you just accept it and move on.

Or the times I missed out on work promotions, I would just assume someone smarter than me got the position, instead of going to ask questions about why I wasn't suited for the position. I looked at people with titles such as teachers, lawyers, doctors, etc. As better than me I felt intimidated being in their presence. I never felt like I measured up. After all, I was 'a nobody' and didn't have anything attached to my name; I was simply a deli assistant in a supermarket. There was nothing special about that, this was a job I got because I dropped out of school and couldn't get anything better. Little did I realize that every time I just accepted these things in my life, I was burying another hurt, disappointed, or angry emotion that was just festering inside me and that one day would rise within me like a volcano that had a lid on it, simmering slowly, waiting for the right moment to explode and purge all that was inside. It is not until we are willing to question our thoughts and feelings and are willing to let go of the things that hold us back from living a fulfilled life that we truly know what it means to accept. The thing is we are not meant to look like everyone else, or think like others think, or feel like others feel; we are all unique in our own way.

The similarities we have with others are that we all think, feel, have a body, have a vision and have a voice. However, we have our own thoughts and feelings, our own vision and voice and a body that is different in size and shape from anyone else's. And that's OK, this is our own personal life and story, but when we measure our own worth by the body and standards of others and accept those standards as the way it should be, we sell ourselves short of our own gifts. Until we learn to accept our own uniqueness, we will always struggle with ourselves. Believing that others are so much more than we could ever be, we look at magazines and believe the models in these books are representative of how we are all meant to look, so we measure our own bodies by those standards without thinking about whether these pictures are real or photo-shopped, which happens a lot these days. Or, we watch reality shows and think that being famous is the way to go, so we search for fame. Today's technology gives people plenty of opportunities to exploit themselves for the world to see.

Life gives us so many experiences, some are bitter pills to swallow and hard to accept, like the loss of a loved one and at times these losses are in horrendous ways, like an illness or disease that leaves us with a disability. It might be losing all our possessions and home in a fire, etc. In these instances, we have to find away to accept so we are able to move forward in life. Acceptance does not mean "I am overweight and unhealthy oh well that's *the* way I am" or "I guess this job will do at least I'm getting paid;' acceptance is admitting that "yes, I have a weight problem and because of that my health is not good, so what can I do to change that?" Or, "This is the only work I could find at the moment, it will give me a chance to earn some money and support myself until I find work that I really enjoy doing." This is accepting and acknowledging things as they are, yet taking responsibility for the changes that are needed to improve the situation.

When we struggle or refuse to accept and acknowledge the way things are, we block our way forward, which leads to anger, frustration and constant disappointment. However, when we accept and acknowledge things as they are, even when we don't like them, we are then able to take the steps we need to move forward and we empower ourselves and create space for great things to happen in our lives, instead of playing small and feeling like a victim of our circumstances.

Take a look at your own life and situation and ask yourself if you are resisting accepting the way things are.

Resistance presents as denial or a sense of feeling helpless, "Poor me". We all have the power within us to create great things and go on to live very fulfilled lives, empowering not just ourselves but the people around us when we accept and acknowledge who and how we are in this very moment. I know that every time I choose to accept and acknowledge all things about myself, I make way for greatness and joy to flow in my life.

What are you ready and willing to accept about yourself?

What are you accepting in your life right now that is preventing you from being the best that you can be?

Lucy Pignataro

Living your best life can only be done when we accept and acknowledge all that we are in the here and now.

God *bless*

CHAPTER 3
Fear

Fear was another major mountain that I needed to climb if I was ever going to move forward and change what needed to be change and understood.

In the English dictionary, fear means "an unpleasant emotion caused by coming danger- be afraid; regard with fear."

So, fear is our perception of possible impending danger, which may or may not happen. There is a possibility of something happening, but most times our fears don't manifest.

The question that comes to mind when I think about fear is, "does it serve a purpose?" and "did it serve a purpose in my journey?"

This is what I know for sure! Fear can be our friend or it can be our enemy, it can propel us forward or it can paralyze us. It can turn something beautiful into something ugly.

Fear can be a motivating force that inspires us into action to do something we have never done before, to find a strength we never knew we had, or it can take hold and grip us like a thief in the night so we feel like we can't breathe and suck every last drop of courage from our being, leaving us reeling with anxiety and panic attacks, unable to function or think clearly. Fear has a way of bringing out the very best in us, or the worst. It can be a warning bell that saves us from impending dangers, or it can wreak havoc, creating a life of hell. I often think about the fear I have experienced in my own life and the opportunities I passed up because of fear, as well as the many times I withdrew from life because I didn't feel I had the courage to move forward.

I had fear that I wasn't good enough, fear of judgment and fear of getting hurt. Did any of these things happen? Would they have happened? I don't know, because I didn't give myself a chance to find out. Instead, I sat on the fence, because wondering "What if?" seemed safer. I always told myself the opportunity would come around again. Some did and others were never heard of again.

There have also been times when a strong sense of fear has saved me. I recall going to a party where I instinctively felt uncomfortable, but wasn't sure why, since nothing seemed threatening.

Several others turned up with drugs and I knew to get out. There was another time when I was offered a business in a seedy part of town and the fear I felt when I parked my car and walked to the place made me think twice about taking it on.

There were times when I wanted something so badly and the fear to go after it was so strong, yet I rose to the challenge and faced my fears one step at a time, until I reached my goal.

There will always be times in our lives when fear will raise its head, nudging us to either move forward or pull back. How many times have you let fear steal from your own life? We were not meant to endure lives of nothing but pain and suffering, with panic and anxiety, where fear has become greater than the joy of living a peaceful and encouraging life. I know I experienced my fair share of anxiety every time I had to face another challenge or confront another obstacle. At times, I had to move away from things or friends that I knew were no longer serving for my greater purpose.

I guess one could say the world we live in gives us many things to fear, such as 9/11 and ongoing terrorist attacks. With all the natural disasters, Tsunamis, earthquakes, torrential rains, blazing fires, planes crashing and car accidents, it's fair to say if we want to focus on fear, there are a lot of things in the world that can fuel it and leave us reeling in fear.

Fortunately, a lot of us may never have to experience any of these things, yet in our heads and with constant media bombardment, we live with it every day. "What if this happens? What if I venture out and get hit by a bus? What if there is a tsunami?" What if this happens, what if that. Is it any wonder so many are suffering from anxiety and panic in today's society?

Antidepressants have become as popular as sugar in our coffee. Do we all allow these incidents to take from us the ability to live peaceful lives? only if we let them.

There is an upside of all these disasters and I believe there will always be an upside; there has to be an upside because that is how life works: night and day, hot and cold, sunshine and rain, life has a way of creating a balance. Fear is no different, with fear comes courage.

I need to question if all these incidents have made us more aware, more conscious of the world we live in and how we live in it. Have we taken life too lightly, given up responsibility in place of personal fulfillment, or believed we were invincible?

Did we all become so complacent and ignorant that we needed a wake-up call (or a few wake up calls)? How many of us have forgotten the importance of family and friends? Let's face it; divorce has become so easy these days you can just about buy one over the counter.

And whatever happened to "love thy neighbour?" If yours is anything like mine, they don't even want us to look their way (sad but true). When was the last time you stopped to help a stranger in trouble? It used to be only children we needed to warn about stranger danger; now we're warning anyone who'll listen.

We are constantly bombarded by road rage. Have we all forgotten how to share and that we are not the only ones on our roads? And why do we think our lives are more important than anyone else's and that somehow gives us the right to be rude and disrespectful to others? Where have the manners we were taught growing up gone?

How many of us saw these events as a wake-up call and decided it was time to change our lives and take stock of what is really important in our lives? How many have been gripped by the fear that life and this world is something to be afraid of and have chosen to withdraw from life?

We live life on antidepressants and in isolation, too afraid to venture out for fear of what might happen.

We all know many people lost their lives and others lost loved ones, lives were torn apart, a lot of people experienced unimaginable pain and torment. Nothing will ever be the same for them and nothing will bring back their loved ones; but when we allow the fear of these circumstances to consume who we are and leave us grappling in a world of panic and anxiety, then their loss and pain has been for nothing.

It doesn't have to be like this. We can honour all those lost lives by changing ours, not by numbing them with medication, but by facing our greatest fears, looking deep within and bringing forth the courage we all have within us and staring fear in the face, unafraid of the battle to overcome it.

I'm not saying it will be easy. It wasn't easy each time I had to face another fear, but I had to believe that I and we have all we need within us to face this battle and overcome our fears. For those who can't do it alone, there are many experienced people who are equipped to help them. Others will discover an inner strength they didn't know was there. Either way, you won't know what you will find until you face it. I, for one, will not allow fear to define my life anymore; I now take opportunities as they present themselves. I have become more mindful of others when I'm sharing our roads and I choose not to be in such a hurry to get to places. And I've taken to smiling and acknowledging others when I'm out on my walks or shopping, even if no one acknowledges or smiles back. I have found most people welcome the smile and do smile back.

I'm learning not to be afraid to ask for help when I need it. No man is an island and there's no shame in asking or offering a helping hand when I see a need. When every one of us faces our own personal fears, I believe we create a ripple effect and begin to change the world around us.

Just for a moment, think about the disasters that we all witnessed and just for a moment, let go of the fear that was felt when you watched it all unfold. Think about all the greatness that came during and after the events, the lives that were united, strangers coming together, caring for each other, open displays of affection and courage in buckets. Hard hearts softened. People united as never before, not allowing fear to define or consume them.

Lives were changed. Many didn't know how strong they were until they were forced by circumstances to face their worst fears. I didn't know what I was capable of until I faced my fears. Fear taught me to live more consciously. New ways of living were discovered because many faced their fears. Many reunited with their families and others started new ones. Others created new jobs, or gave up old ones. Some took on jobs they never imagined they would do.

Countries stood united, offering assistance in many different ways. New ways of being emerged.

In so much sadness and destruction, fear showed us all sides of itself. The good, the bad, the ugly and the beautiful.

Fear showed us the human spirit at its absolute very best and continues to reveal the very best of the human spirit as these events will continue to unfold for many years to come, bringing more and more change and unity in and around us.

So back to the original question: does fear serve a purpose?

In some instances, I believe it does serve a purpose and can be just as important as the need for love and in some cases. Fear is what actually brings love to the surface.

An element of fear is needed to keep us motivated and gently propel us forward. At the same time, there is a need for awareness so that we are not consumed by fear to the point of not being able to move forward.

Be brave enough to feel the fear and do it anyway. Chances are the worst thing may never happen.

As a human race, I believe we will continue to experience incidents in the world that will challenge us at our core and that's not a bad thing. Throughout our lives, it is inevitable that we will experience many different emotions along with the challenges we will face, the lesson is learning how to allow these emotions to move through us and teach us about our human spirit and what we are capable of. Or, we can allow these emotions to paralyze and define us and limit our own greatness to make a difference in the world we live in.

Think of how many times you have let fear hold you back or keep you stuck in a life that made or makes you miserable.

Are you living a life dictated by other people's rules and regulations because fear won't let you trust your own spirit to guide you? How many of you are in jobs or relationships that are not bringing out the very best of who you were meant to be, but you are too afraid to take a leap of faith and try something different?

Every minute of our lives is an opportunity to step into our greater selves and live without fear. If you keep doing what you have always done, you will keep getting what you've got; be brave and try something new.

Step out of the fear that chains you. You have a choice and don't let anyone or anything tell you that you don't. The greatest life you will ever live may just be a breath away, are you ready to take it and fly?

The choice is always ours. What will you choose?

God bless

Chapter 4
Anger

Anger was a very confronting emotion. I had no idea I could hold so much anger within me. It is such a passionate word and can stir up such intense emotion.

It can rage like a torrent of water gushing out from us in bucket loads, or it can be so passive and silent, and then catch us unaware and erupt like a volcano when we least expect. When I look back on the anger that erupted from me when I least expected, it was a buildup of years of saying "yes" when I really wanted to say "no," all the times I tried to use my voice and was shut down by those around me, all the years of not feeling valued no matter what I did and the constant put-downs that I never stood up to.

Anger can fire us up so that we will defend our beliefs with such intensity and passion that others will be forced to sit up, listen and pay attention. Or, it can clear a room in seconds, making everyone run for cover.

Anger can be so destructive and disempowering, impacting people's lives and leaving them traumatized and fearful for great lengths of time. Some of my anger came from many years of being at the receiving end of other people's anger.

What is it about anger that can get us so fired up and enraged, blinding us to any rational behaviour?

How many times have you allowed your anger to spew out on to others, sometimes innocent victims who had no part in what made you so angry in the first place?

How many times have you been left red-faced because you allowed your anger to get the better of you and someone dared to hold you accountable for your behaviour?

How many times have you tried to convince yourself or others that the anger you feel is justified?

How many relationships have been destroyed or strained because you didn't restrain your anger, but instead shared it around like you were giving out chocolates, expecting everyone to just take it?

Does anger give us the right to behave so badly towards others?

So many have and continue to suffer at the hands of others who have no control of their anger. This is anger that is out of control and destructive. Then there is anger that can create shifts without the destruction; and, while I don't advocate anger, there are times when the only way to break free of the barriers we erected throughout our lives is to find our voice and stand up for ourselves. And sometimes that voice can come forward quite strongly. When this happens, it becomes a benchmark to rethink what it is that we are actually feeling and become aware of our emotional state. Is this the same as venting anger at the drop of a hat? For me it made me aware that I was capable of getting angry and that I needed to learn how to express that anger safely and effectively. Why is it that we get angry? What triggers the anger?

Now that I have a greater understanding of what anger is, when I look at what it is that gets me fired up, it is an unmet desire! Yep, I wanted something to happen that didn't or I wanted someone to do something my way and they didn't.

At other times, it was expecting others to see things my way as though it was the only way.

When we have a desire for something or an expectation of something or someone, we have a preconceived idea of what we want to happen, so we put so much energy and attention into what we want. We don't stop to think, "Is the other person aware of what I want?"

Are they capable of delivering what we want? Are we even aware that we are imposing this desire onto a situation or individual? Most of the time, if we think about it, we just want what we want, without any for thought of who or what will be affected by it.

Then, when we don't get the outcome we want, we become angry. Some become very angry, even to the point of violence, when they physically lash out at someone. Does anger have a place in the world we live in?

I believe anger that is kept in check can be a very constructive emotion that can create great shifts in people, if it is delivered in an appropriate manner.

When I say appropriate manner, it is to acknowledge that we are feeling angry, also to recognize what it is that we had desired and didn't get and take responsibility for our part. We then need to ask ourselves, "What other way can I get my desire met without negatively affecting others?" I have also found it helpful to discuss with the other person what I'm feeling.

To share our feelings of anger does not mean that we get to put others down or belittle them to prove a point, or to determine who is right or wrong. It is too simply state: "in this situation, this is what I was expecting and because that expectation was not met, I now feel angry." Breathe, this is a great way to release the anger. For me, just being given the space to have my say and be listened to is enough for me to move past my anger.

We all have our own way of dealing with the energy of our anger. We need to remember that anger is just that 'an energy', just like sadness and every other emotion in our lives and all our anger expects from us is that it be acknowledged.

Continual practice of being aware when we get angry and coming back to our unmet expectation provides an opening to release the energy without anyone getting hurt or caught up in the anger.

Sometimes the flare-up of anger means that new boundaries need to be set. Maybe at some point throughout our lives it became normal to react with anger because that is what we saw being modelled by our peers, so it has become a bad habit that needs to be changed. Sometimes anger became a way to protect ourselves, like a defense mechanism.

Anger, if expressed effectively, can express passion for something of importance that might make a difference to the lives of many. There may even be times when anger has saved us from a threatening predator.

Anger is a natural human emotion and it affects each of us in different ways. Anger does not have to be destructive; it need not shatter the lives of others or our own for that matter. What's important is that we become aware and mindful of how we choose to feel and express our anger. When we choose to ignore the signs of anger in our bodies and suppress it, thinking it will just go away, we are usually caught unaware as it rears its ugly head at an inappropriate time. I discovered this the hard way. Have you ever had an accident and wondered, "Why did that happen?" Think for a minute and reflect on your state of mind just before the accident. Is it possible you were holding on to anger that you had ignored and now the accident is trying to bring it to your attention? Don't kid yourself into believing, "If I don't think about what I'm feeling, it will just disappear," because it won't. It is just sitting in waiting for the appropriate moment to return to your attention. Energy needs an outlet; it needs to keep moving and it can't move effectively if we refuse to acknowledge that it is there.

How are you going to deal with your anger when it flares up? Will you be willing to find a constructive way to let it go? Anger does not have to control your life, nor do you need to wear it like a shield. Find safe, effective ways to release your anger. Sometimes just the fact that we acknowledge our anger and learn to witness the energy in our bodies and keep breathing consciously is enough to release the anger. It ultimately comes down to awareness and choice.

We are all role models for each other; be someone who leads by example and together we can create a peaceful world.

God Bless

CHAPTER 5
Trust

This was another issue that was continually challenging me to look at and understand at a deeper level. I trusted people so blindly, only to find myself continually hurt and disappointed. So I spent a fair amount of time contemplating trust.

What does it mean to trust someone or to be trusted by others? Trust, by definition, means firm reliance on the integrity and ability of a person or thing.

Why do we trust people? And when we do trust people, do we have an expectation of that trust in return? If so, would you still call it trust, control, or expectation? Interesting, isn't it?

Let's look at what it means to put your trust in someone. For me, it means that I have faith in that person and the way they interact in my life, to do the right thing according to what I believe to be right, e.g. not to take from me, or hurt me, to be dependable, have integrity and be there for me. I trust that they won't lie and I trust that they will always be honest with me.

When I was younger and really didn't understand trust, I guess I just believed without much thought that the people in my life would do the right thing. As a child, I trusted that my parents would love me and provide for me until I would be able to look after myself. Throughout my teenage years, I trusted that my friends would always like me and be friendly and naively that boys would always treat me well. At work, I trusted that if I showed up and worked, I would be paid. Now, as an adult life, has given me many experiences, so I contemplate trust and ask myself, "Should we just blindly trust the people that come into our lives, just because they might be friendly or because they are family?"

Should we just trust people because they tell us they are trustworthy? In a marriage or relationships, should we just trust our partner because we love them and have married them? Again do we just trust our children because we gave birth to them and brought them into the world and raised them? Should we just trust our parents because they brought us into the world and raised us and provided for us? Does that make them trustworthy? Should business partners be trusted because we both have a vested interest and believe we have the same goal in mind for our business?

In my life I have experienced all of the above. In one relationship, my partner cheated and showed me he was not trustworthy to honour our relationship. Just because there was love didn't mean there would be trust. I have

In Search of my Soul

children who at times have shown themselves to be not trustworthy. There have been times in my life that I trusted my parents to be there and support me, only to have them do the complete opposite. I have been in business where my partner refused to honour an agreement, once the business was running.

In these experiences, trust didn't shine through; instead, it was lessons that showed me that I took for granted that all these people were important in my life and therefore trustworthy.

So was the lesson that I was too trusting? or that I needed to understand what it means to trust someone?

I would say in these instances that I did assume that I could trust these people because of my association with them, only to learn that trust is something that needs to be earned and not expected or taken for granted. Just because someone tells me they love me doesn't mean that I should blindly trust them. It will be through the course of the relationship that trust is built and earned. Saying that does not necessarily mean that, once trust is established, it is set in stone and it will never be tested. The same with our children; just because we gave birth to them and raised them (and don't get me wrong, I adore my children,) does not mean they are trustworthy. Trust is something they need to understand and earn. Again, this happens through life experiences and what we teach them along the way.

Even once we feel that they are trustworthy, it cannot be taken for granted that the trust we have in them will never be challenged. The same goes for our parents, there will be times when we do take it for granted that we trust them to do what we want or need. Business partners! Friendship is one thing, working that closely is another and requires a lot of honesty and integrity to trust each other, Sometimes trust seems a lot easier in theory than it is in actuality.

The practicality is very different. Think about the people in your life: friends, family, work colleagues, neighbours; and consider the relationship you have with these people. Now ask yourself if there is trust. Do you trust these people and are you trustworthy in these relationships? Do you take that trust for granted or have you blindly trusted that these relationships have integrity? Have these people earned your trust in them? And have you earned their trust in you? When that trust is betrayed, how many of us say "I trusted you and you betrayed that trust?" Did we ever earn that trust in each other, or was it just expected that, because of the relationship, that trust should be there. There are things in life that we can trust blindly. Such as that the sun will rise every day. It may not shine through the clouds every day. But rest assured it will rise. We can trust that the moon will also rise every night; again, just because we can't always see it doesn't mean it isn't there. These things we can trust without fear of being hurt or disappointed.

However, it seems that trust is another one of those qualities that needs to be learned and explored and experienced in order to understand why it is important in our lives.

So many of us go through our lives without really thinking about our place in the lives of others and their place in our lives. We always assume that somehow being in the same family, being friends or business partners, husbands, or wives, that trust somehow comes with the relationship. Yet I'm here to tell you that it doesn't; trust is a quality that needs to be built, earned by the value we place on our relationships and built with honesty and integrity.

There are times when we can justify to ourselves that breaking that trust was done so as not to hurt the other person or to save the other person in some way. In these instances, careful consideration needs to be taken of the outcome of breaking that trust. While we assume that we know what is best for the other person that may not necessarily be the case.

What about the trust we have in ourselves? Do you trust yourself? By that, I mean do you trust the decisions you make, or do you second -guess yourself or ask others for their opinions and base your decision on what they might say?

Are you aware of the feeling within yourself that is trying to get your attention, but you ignoring it because you don't trust yourself or your instincts?

What about when your spirit is trying to guide you? Would you trust that subtle voice that gently offers direction and guidance? How many opportunities have you missed because you didn't trust that voice? How many times have things in your life not worked out because you chose to listen to someone else rather than follow the voice of your spirit?

I will be the first to admit that, at times, I chose not to listen to my spirit and suffered the consequences.

Lucy Pignataro

I have found trust to be one of qualities I struggled with more than others. I was too trusting of others and not trusting enough of myself; and there has never been a shortage of lessons to teach me to find the balance.

What I have found works best is to be aware as much as possible of the feelings that arise in our body. When trust is in question, our gut instincts will warn us with tightness in the abdomen, or it might feel like a jolt. With practice, you will become familiar with your body's warning signs. Think about what your spirit might be trying to draw your attention to and trust whatever comes up. Our instincts are rarely wrong. It is important that we can trust the people in our lives, but most of all, it is important to trust ourselves.

If we learn to trust ourselves, then we are more aware when trust in others needs to be questioned.

The next time your spirit tries to get your attention, trust yourself enough to listen to what it's trying to tell you and if you are still not sure, sit quietly and become aware of the sensations in your body. Do you feel light and free, or do you feel tight and rigid? In time and with practice, you will know very clearly, without doubt. There will undoubtedly be times when you get it wrong and that's OK, don't give up, keep practicing; you will get there. Our lives become very empowering when we learn to trust our spirit and follow its guidance.

God bless

Chapter 6
Forgiveness

Along the way, I learned that forgiveness is a very important quality if I was going to heal and make peace with myself, along my journey, not being able to forgive just kept me stuck. I found forgiveness to be quite a strong word and one that would make a big difference in my life. It certainly carries a lot of power. It can make or break us, depending on how or if we choose to use it.

What does it really mean to forgive? Why is it so important to forgive? Who is it important for?

Let's first take look at what it isn't. To forgive does not mean we are giving up or giving in. It is not saying it's OK to hurt me. It's not a sign of defeat or weakness. It is not justifying another's behaviour or making allowances for abuse of any kind. I believe to forgive is to give ourselves permission to heal and make peace within our being.

It is gives us permission to heal and to set ourselves free.

Free of the pain that we have endured and carried with us, like a shackle holding us firmly in one place, through the behaviour of another that hurt us in some way.

We are all human and in the act of being human, we will hurt each other, our children will hurt us, our husbands and wives will hurt us, our siblings and parents will hurt us, friends and bosses will hurt us and sometimes strangers will hurt us, at times by accident and sometimes intentionally.

"To be hurt by someone accidently" means there was no intention to set out to hurt anyone. Maybe this is what is said to be "in the wrong place at the wrong time."

When this happens, the person that caused the hurt is usually filled with remorse for their actions. It seems to be easier to forgive someone who is suffering for what they did as much as we are suffering from pain of their actions. Then there are the times when the experience that caused our pain was intentional; that's when forgiving becomes a real challenge.

Rolled into our pain and hurt is usually anger. We are angry with the person who hurt us; we are angry that we put ourselves in the path to be hurt; there are all sorts of reasons why we are angry.

When someone intentionally sets out to cause pain and suffering to another, the consequence of this behaviour usually leaves the person feeling intense and reeling, trying to make sense of what just happened and why!

Can you remember a time when you were hurt by someone? And if you were asked, what would you need to get past the hurt to be able to forgive?

Most of us would probably say we want revenge, we want to see them punished and hurting the way we are hurting.

We want them to know what they have done, how pissed we are, how much were hurting because of their actions. But if we were to be really honest with ourselves, would that help us get through the pain? Would it really make us feel better? Would it set us free of our pain? How would someone hurting release us from our pain?

As much as I like to say it would make me feel better, it really doesn't because I don't get any pleasure or satisfaction out of seeing anyone hurting. Do you?

Now let's think about this for a minute. Someone has caused us pain; we feel anger, hurt and maybe suffering as a result of the experience. The thoughts of this experience keep playing out over and over in our head and we just can't seem to get past it. We refuse to forgive the other person; we decide we will never forget what happened, never forget what they did to us.

This whole thought pattern seems to attach itself to our being, so that every time we see the person or something that reminds us of the hurt, we are thrown back to the scene. It feels like an open wound that has bled, but never healed, continually getting infected and oozing out and we keep mopping it up and applying another band-aid, until the next time. The other thing to think about is: "How many other people around us are affected by our thoughts of not being able to forgive?" Let's face it, when we are angry or hurting, don't we all have a way of letting others know how we feel?

Another way of putting it is: imagine the person who hurt you! You have captured them (because you know who they are) and you put them in a prison cell and lock the door and you sit outside watching them, because you swear you will never forgive them or forget what they did to you.

And you pace up and down, making sure there's no way out and they are not going to get away with it.

Think about this carefully, and then ask yourself, "Who is the real prisoner here? Now, before you walk away in frustration, let's put this in perceptive.

As I said in the beginning, to forgive does not mean it's OK for you to hurt me, nor is it giving in.

It is acknowledging the pain, anger and hurt that we feel; it is looking at ourselves and being brave enough to ask, "Why did I choose to have this experience?" Maybe we are the kind of person who always put other people's needs before our own, making their lives and emotions more important than ours. Maybe the only way for us to see this was to have someone hurt us, so that we can then begin to change how we see ourselves and others and to heal that part of ourselves that at some point in our journey decided others were more important than me.

So to forgive is to forgive yourself of this way of being and to never forget is to remind yourself that you are a valuable human being who has feelings and emotions that are just as important as others and I will not put myself in situations where I make myself or my feelings of lesser value or importance than others.

Now we can begin to heal and make peace with ourselves. Now we can release the grip of pain, anger and our inability to forgive. It is not for us to be accountable for the actions of others; only they can be responsible for what they put out into the universe. We all plant our own seeds and they will only sprout what we sowed into them.

Everything that happens to us serves a purpose; that purpose is not always clear or pleasant. Remember, we have come to this earth to learn, grow and evolve as human beings. We are here to learn how to live in love and in order for that to happen; we need to know what love isn't so that we can know what love is. In order for us to understand what it means to really forgive, we have to experience hurt and pain then reflect to discover the art of forgiveness.

When we can't, or choose not to, look for the grace in our experience, we suffer, not only from the painful experience, but from our own resistance to change and learn.

Forgiveness is in no way justification for the way some people behave; however, everything comes with the grace of learning from experiences, even the most painful ones.

The thing is that if we cannot make peace, with ourselves and those who gave us the experience of pain it is our bodies that bear the brunt of carrying the pain that eats away at us. As long as we live, there will always be someone or something that will cause us pain. Forgiveness leads to true health and happiness; our experiences are our teachers that provide the opportunities for happiness, peace and love. I hope you can: find your way to forgive and not to let your experience consume you or define who you are, that you are able to see yourself as someone greater than your pain.

Choose to make peace with yourself, because that is where true freedom lies. I will not say that it is easy, but if we are to heal and learn, it is important that we at least give it a try. Some things will be easier to forgive than others; however, if you continually remind yourself that forgiveness is for your wellbeing, you will get there.

God bless

Chapter 7
Giving

Giving has taught me a lot about the quality of life I wanted to live and how to harness the essence that comes from giving.

What does it mean to give? When you give, is it unconditionally or is it out of obligation, or because you expect something in return? How can we learn to give unconditionally? And what exactly does unconditional giving mean?

To give means to apply oneself (there were many definitions in the dictionary). We can give of our time, our thoughts, or we can give something material, give our love, our blessing, our energy. It all depends on who or what we are giving to. Does that change the way in which we give?

Every day, in some way, we are all giving; and that is a wonderful thing. However, what is the state of your heart when you are in the act of giving? Have you or do you think about your state of mind when you give?

I know a lot of you are probably thinking that I ask a lot of questions and I do; because, without the questions, I cannot come to know myself or the true value of my life.

Again, giving was not something I gave a lot of thought to when I was growing up. I just did what came naturally and I have a very generous spirit. While it is a wonderful quality, it certainly became one that I needed to contemplate and gain a better understanding of.

Giving is not about keeping score, such as I gave to you now you owe. It is so much more than we have ever really thought about. It was certainly something that taught me a lot about myself, others and the way I live my life. I love that I have this great capacity to give and help others; it can be very enriching and rewarding to both the giver and receiver. However, on the down side, it can drain the life out me and leave me feeling empty and exhausted.

For years, I was not aware that this was the cause of a lot of what I was feeling and it wasn't until I started to take a greater interest in myself and the way I lived my life, that I realized what I was doing and that things had to change.

I was definitely a "yes girl:" "can you do this?" "Yes" "can you go there?" "Yes?" My life seemed to be a series of yeses to everything and everyone. I was generous with my time, generous with my thoughts, generous with my feelings, generous with gifts, generous with obligation and duty. I was Miss Dependable and always reliable.

Come hell or high water, I would always deliver. For many years, I didn't think I knew the word 'no' existed. At some point, I realized something had to change. There seemed to be a great imbalance in my life and while I enjoyed giving to others, I would often feel angry and frustrated and did not understand why.

The best way to describe it is: imagine going to the bank daily and making large deposits in other people's accounts; but, when you go to withdraw from your own account, it is empty.

Do you blame others? No, there really is no one to blame, just lessons that need to learned about the art of giving and what it really means to give.

So, I started to pay attention. When someone wanted my time, before I jumped in boots and all, I took a moment.

That great pause is such a saving grace.

What was my state? Did it sit right in my body to give in this moment, or did my body feel rigid and contracted? Did it feel right in my heart? Who would benefit from me giving my time at this point? I started to see that if it didn't feel right in my body, then it was important for all concerned that I acknowledge and honour that feeling and say "no."

It was important because when I continually say "yes" and I really want to say "no," I am interfering with natural laws of the universe. Maybe the person asking needs to be more responsible in their own life and me giving to them in that moment stops them from learning. There may be all sorts of lessons to be learned and when we keep doing what we have always done, we will keep getting the same result and nothing is learned. However, when we rock the boat and do something different, we start to learn and grow and allow others to learn their own lessons.

What about being generous with our emotions? When we share so openly with others and continually do so without thinking about what we are putting out, it becomes like verbal diarrhoea, it is exhausting for the person/people listening and exhausting for the person talking. There is no benefit to anyone and it can actually keep you stuck in your emotional drama. But when we think before we speak and take into consideration the impact our words can have on all concerned, we learn to speak from a space of healing that frees us from our drama rather than fuels it. We give out inspiration and respect for ourselves and others.

Have you thought about the state you are in when you share your emotional state? Do you just want to talk or do you want to be able to let it go and heal? Do you want empathy or sympathy? One will support you to heal; the other will keep you playing the victim.

When I share my emotional state now, I do so with a willingness to help others deal with their emotional dramas, therefore providing inspiration instead of pity. This uplifts others rather than drains and burdens them with unnecessary drama. You can check this out for yourself; when you are out with friends, do you come home feeling heavy and agitated or do you come home feeling uplifted and content and can honestly say, "I enjoyed my time with my friends?"

Other ways in which we give to others is in gifts. When you buy a gift for someone, do you buy with a loving and generous heart, or do you buy out of obligation and annoyance? Let's just clear up that a generous heart does not mean "I need to spend a lot of money," it means, "I really want to give this person a gift that expresses how important they are in my life."

So I take into account what that person means to me and what sort of gift best expresses that. Sometimes it's a candle to reflect the light they bring to my life, or a bunch of colorful flowers to reflect the beauty of their nature. It might be a nice bottle of wine to celebrate the special times we've had together. It is in giving from this place that I am able to give up expectation of a returned gift. The blessing is that the gift is received with the loving spirit that it is given.

Giving a gift without thought or feeling is usually received in the same spirit: it was given without love and no one's life was enriched through the experience.

What about receiving? How do you receive the gifts given to you? Have you also noticed the times that you give and seem to do it so freely, yet when someone tries to give you something, you find it hard to receive? Why do you think that is?

Why is it so easy for some to give, yet they don't know how to or allow themselves receive? Isn't that sending a message that others are more deserving and that we are not worthy to receive help, gifts, complements, etc?

When this happens, how does the giving benefit anyone? The more we become aware of our state when it comes to giving, the greater the joy we feel when we give with a loving heart. The saying 'to give is to receive' is so true and being open to receiving when others give to us can be just as rewarding and healing for the giver and the receiver.

Lucy Pignataro

When we let go of the expectation to get something back every time we give, we end up receiving in so many other ways. The returned gift of giving does not necessarily come back through the same person. When our vessel of receiving is expected to be the person we gave to, we will often be left feeling empty and disappointed. So, I say give with an open heart, without any expectation and know you are helping love to circulate. When you look at a circle, there is no end, just a circle that goes around and around. You will also be teaching others how to follow your lead and you begin to receive in ways you have never thought if. Giving can open the heart and spread love faster than a blazing fire and for the receiver, it can melt a stony heart. So the next time you are about to give in some way, put some thought into how you are going give. You will be surprised the difference it can make in your life and the lives of others and start to become aware how much better you feel. This is another great quality that opens our heart and helps us to feel free instead of feeling constantly drained by giving without thought.

God bless

CHAPTER 8
Courage

Courage, by definition in the dictionary, means "boldness, bravery, fortitude and daring."

It's not a word like to take lightly. It's a word that can stir fear in the hearts of some and give rise to power in others.

For me, it has played such a major part in my life journey and transformed so much in me. At one point, courage would always stir up a lot of fear, making me run for cover and withdraw, unless it was a life or death situation where

I did it have time to think about what I was feeling and just needed to be courageous and do what needed to be done.

However, the journey to reconnect with my soul has made me dig deep and find the courage within and learn to trust that I had the ability to be courageous. Drawing on my courageous side wasn't always easy. Many times, when the fear would paralyze me and I didn't know how to move forward, I had no choice but to find the courage within me and face my fears and the challenges in front of me. I recall when I felt like my world was caving in. I was experiencing things I had never felt before and nothing made any sense and I didn't know what to do or where to turn and I wasn't sure I wanted to go on. The desperation I felt was so frightening that I would pray so hard for courage, courage to find help, courage to believe that I could somehow get through this darkness. Many times, there was another mountain to climb and another barrier to break down. It took courage to find my voice and use it. It took courage to believe in myself; to push past all the obstacles and find fulfillment in my life. It took courage to face life after the loss of my father; we don't realize how much we depend on our parents' advice or guidance, even when we don't always agree with it. Then, there are times when it took courage to be still and have faith that all will be well. So many times, when courage was called for and I found it every time, it was always there within me, waiting to serve me. I just needed to become aware that it was and always will be within me. I have found the courage to write this book and share my life with others. There was a time when I could not even allow myself to think about doing something like this and yet here I am. Every time I found the courage to be true to myself, I felt so much freedom and contentment within my being. For many years, I hid behind a mask of fear, believing I could never be brave enough to follow my heart, only to live a miserable and discontented life. I passed up a lot of opportunities because I believed I never had the courage to do what was asked of

In Search of my Soul

me. It took me a long time to find my voice and live my truth. It has been through life experiences that my voice became clearer and louder and not shut down by fear.

It was all because I felt I didn't have the courage and I was afraid of the rejection by others. Courage is never far away. It is always right there inside us, to draw on when we need it. So many people believe they don't have the courage it takes to surmount the obstacles that life can throw at us, only to find themselves in situations where their courage shines through like a beacon of light, surprising even them.

Courage is not something that we can buy or take or that can even be given to us by others; courage is a part of who we are. It is in our DNA. Most of us have just buried it so far down that we convince ourselves that we don't have it, like it is something others have that somehow we weren't given at birth. Sometimes courage is not visible to the human eye or felt in our being; courage is a virtue that at times you need to dig out, dust it off and then use it where it needs to be used. Sometimes courage rises up to meet us when we least expect it. In moments of terror, when we may find ourselves dealing with life-or-death situations, courage may find you when you need to find your voice and stand up for something you believe in. The times when life throws you a curve ball and you just don't think you can keep going, trust me when I tell you that courage is there to help you, one step at a time. You will get past whatever seems impossible. As long as there is life, there will always be possibilities; you need courage to seek them out.

We always hear stories of bravery and courage, of people saving the lives of others in terrible situations, of children standing up to the people that bully them.

Courage is not getting angry at others to boast about how great you are. Courage is not putting your life or the lives of others in dangerous situations to show off or prove a point.

Courage can sometimes be very subtle, such as having the courage to do something kind for another. Or the courage it takes to look into your own heart and see what's there.

Then there is the courage it takes to acknowledge the truth of who we are, knowing that it goes against everything we were raised to believe. When we awaken the courage within ourselves, we start to live a life of contentment and no longer need to hide behind our fears. Sometimes it takes courage to just do nothing and trust that all will be taken care of. What does courage mean to you? And how do you display courage? Take the time to think about courage, do you play small and hide behind fear because you think you could never be brave? It doesn't serve you and anybody else for you to play small and insignificant. Find the courage within you to break free of this pattern; you will inspire others to do the same. Know that we can all make a difference when we find the courage within us to shine and bring light into the world. Finding the courage within me has set me free to be the person I was truly meant to be and fulfill my life purpose. Do you have the courage within you to fulfill your life purpose, whatever that may be?

Courage is not something that you find outside yourself; a contented life comes when you find the courage within, set yourself free, live the life of your dreams and fulfill your purpose.

God Bless

Chapter 9
Love

Love was an emotion that was constantly in question throughout my quest to discover my soul. Why? Because, truth be known, I wasn't sure what love really was. I know people use the word "love" continuously, but what does it really mean and why does it have such a great impact on our lives?

Love, by definition in the English dictionary, means "A strong feeling of affection and sexual attraction for someone," but is that all it is?

One could argue that sexual attraction is a physical desire or attraction and does not necessarily come with feelings of affection.

We could even question whether the strong feeling of affection is love.

Have you ever found yourself questioning the validity of love? What is this thing called love? Does it really exist? Is it real or is it just a fantasy we conjure up in our minds to distract us from the mundane humdrum of our lives? How will I know when I'm in love? How will I find love; or, more to the point, how will love find me?

In Search of my Soul

Why are we told it is so painful when we lose love? And what exactly is it that we lose? Or when we have to let love go? So many questions and all for such a small word 'love'; or so you think!

Do you remember your very first experience of love? Can you recall the way it made you feel? Was it exciting? Did it leave you reeling? Or did it just stop you in your tracks and leave you wondering "What just happened?"

For me, love has never been an experience that didn't affect me in some way.

I can remember my first experience of love. I'm talking about my first conscious experience. I was a five year old; we had just visited family friends and I felt so excited. There was an older man. When I say older, I don't mean old, I mean teenager, remember, I was only 5. I guess for some the feeling strikes young and it didn't feel the same as what

I felt for members of my family. I remember arriving home and I was so excited I declared my undying love for this man, much to my father's horror.

My father was an old-generation Italian and he didn't particularly know how to support or humour a 5-year-old's fantasy of love.

Was it a fantasy? Or was it real? Well, from what I remember, I felt really happy, like I was going to burst at the seams.

I felt butterflies in my stomach and I wanted to tell everyone. I don't ever recall butterflies in my stomach whenever

I saw my family. However, the reception I got from my father soon squashed any feelings or fantasy I had about love and I believe to this day that it also changed my perception of love. It seemed to me that, if it is love, that this feeling should not be shared, because not everyone likes it. Secondly, love seems to carry feelings of shame and embarrassment.

Again, please remember that this was my perception and interpretation. After that experience, I thought twice about rushing into that feeling again. I thought that if I just didn't think about it, I would never have to feel all those feelings again, like I somehow had control over how love operates.

Well, it seems this feeling called love can creep up on us whenever it feels like it. I say this because I don't recall making an effort to go in search of it.

My next experience came in 6th grade. He was the new boy at school and I fell head over heels in love with him and it seemed that I wasn't the only one, so did a lot of other girls in the grade. He was easy on the eye, tall, dark and handsome. Another fact: love creates competition. Sometimes more than one person will fall in love with the same person. It was the same excited feeling, butterflies in the stomach, only this time I wasn't sharing this with anyone. I decided I would sit this one out and hope that he would feel the same and notice me. As love would have it, I missed the boat. He didn't notice me. Next lesson: sometimes you have to fight for love or make a slight scene so the object of your love will take notice.

So, love requires work and effort. This thing called love seems to start off well. The excitement and butterflies in the stomach actually feel good; then it seems to go downhill. Now, I'm not one to be defeated and I believe in giving love second chances, in this case a third chance. At 15 years old I again fell in love and I know at this age when hormones are running rampant, love can be confused with lust and sexual desire. However, on closer inspection, there is a difference.

Love is a longing and an ache that is felt in the heart. Lust is a longing and ache that is felt in the groin.

This time, love was slow to start and I didn't notice it coming, as we started as friends and the feelings gradually grew more intense. This time the love was reciprocated, love was gentle, love was kind, love was caring and love was patient, no pressure.

So far my understanding of love was exciting, shameful, embarrassing, gentle, caring, kind and patient. This thing called love seems to have many facets. Love is not always clearly defined.

I'm now beginning to feel that love is at times challenging, it seems to stir up other feelings within me. Sometimes I feel jealousy and hurt, sometimes anger and frustration. Again, is it love? Or is it the story we tell ourselves about love, such as "if you loved me, you wouldn't do that" or "if you really loved me you would do/ give me, what I want?"

From this it is fair to say that love can be used as a bargaining tool. Love can be manipulated, or used to manipulate another to get what we want.

Is that still love? Well, at 15 years old, I don't think I was equipped or wise enough to really understand the full meaning of the word. However, I do know that most times this thing called love, despite the many facets it comes with, does feel good and, given a choice, I prefer the feeling of love over the feeling of anger.

Does love always need to involve another person? At that time in my life, that is how I experienced love: through my relationship with others. I am now also becoming aware that, in relationships, we can fall out of love with the person we have confessed undying love for not too long ago. Falling out of love with someone isn't the most comfortable feeling, it's just that the excitement and butterflies are becoming fleeting and the ache in the heart becomes dull. The anticipation of seeing the one we supposedly loved is dwindling and we would rather not see them.

This is where we discover that love can hurt. Again, I ask the question, is it love that hurts or the story we tell ourselves about how love should or shouldn't be? Surely, if we no longer have that feeling of love for someone, we can just walk away and some people do, no questions asked. However, there are some of us who struggle with hurting others, so we stay in relationships without love for fear of hurting others, telling ourselves that things will change.

Another thing: we use love to lie to ourselves and others. Then we use love or lack of love to trap ourselves in situations that no longer serve us. So here we find another so-called aspect of love: entrapment!

Another question that I'm sure some of us have thought about, is it possible to love 2 people at once?

While I have never had this experience, I have had friends who would testify to loving 2 people at once, saying that both people had very different personalities and were able to offer different forms of love, both of which felt good.

No one form was better or worse than the other and it was therefore difficult to let go of either one. From this, I would ascertain that we are capable of loving more than one person at a time, if we choose to. So then, do we let love flow in all directions, or do we truly believe that love should only be with one person at a time?

In my opinion, as interesting as it sounds to be able to love two people at once, nurturing one relationship is more than enough for me. (When I talk about nurturing one relationship, I'm talking about an intimate one. Not all the others we have going at the same time, such as the love of our children, parents, friends, etc.) So, therefore, according to some, it is possible to love more than one person at a time. The list seems to keep growing; am I any wiser yet, I don't think so; do I have a greater understanding of love? Not yet. What I do know for sure is that, as we get older, we want different things from love.

We learn to bargain and compromise with love and it is so much more than we imagined it to be. I am now 50 and have been married to the same man for twenty-two years. In this relationship, I have continued to experience all the different faces of love, including the ones I experienced growing up, only this time with the same man. I have learned that it is only through all the different facets of love and allowing that love to teach me, that I can discover what love really is.

Love isn't a story, it isn't even a feeling, love is who we are, all of us expressions of love in many different forms.

Our experiences are meant to peel away the layers that keep our true expression of love hidden. At our core, we are nothing but pure love. Our relationships are the canvas onto which we project that love. So, when we experience turmoil in these relationships, love is looking for a way to realign itself with its purest form.

Without our relationships (both intimate and others), it would be very difficult to know or understand love. All the different kinds, e.g. family, friends and lovers, are avenues to allow love to teach us many things about ourselves.

Sometimes we can experience great love with one person and sometimes it can take many before we allow ourselves to learn from love.

Love will always be in our lives, whether we are aware of it or not; we just need to be present to experience this love.

If we use love to manipulate, it can be destructive and painful; however, if we learn to trust love and allow it to take effect, it can also be our greatest healer. Love can change our whole perception of life, if we are open to it.

Love can bring out the very best of who we are, uniting us in ways we hadn't thought possible. Love doesn't always come in beautiful packages; and, more times than not, love can appear in very strange ways and in places that we least expect to find it; or, more to the point, it finds us.

Love doesn't always come when we want it or think we are ready for it. Love has its own agenda and it won't be rushed by anybody or anything.

In Search of my Soul

So, the next time you feel challenged in your relationships, think about the way your love is trying to realign itself with its purest form, wanting to find expression. Learn to trust the love in your life to guide you, especially in the most challenging moments. Love's plan for us is far more intelligent than anything we can come up with. Learn to be patient with love so that it can teach you. Be still and listen, it will sound like a whisper in the wind, gentle and subtle.

The greatest lesson that love has taught and continues to teach me on this journey is how to love myself, because it is only when I truly love and accept myself that I can truly love another.

God bless

CHAPTER 10
Marriage

For me, my marriage became another major learning ground and it certainly wasn't the fantasy I had dreamed about as a little girl. My marriage was the mirror that reflected back to me all my unresolved pain and shed many more layers that prevented me from loving myself and offering unconditional love.

Marriage, by definition in the English dictionary, is a "union between two people."

Marriage/partnership, what is it all about? Is it about love? Is it about being blissfully happy for the rest of our lives?

Is it about bringing children into the world? I believe it is all of those things and more on many different levels, combined with many different stages.

Does your marriage live up to the expectation you had imagined all those years ago? Is it the wedded bliss you had hoped for? Are you happy with the partner you chose?

In Search of my Soul

There are marriages/partnerships that maybe should never have come together and are detrimental to each other's wellbeing. It takes a lot of courage and honesty with each other to recognize that the best thing for each other's growth is to go separate ways.

Then there are marriages/relationships that have the potential to be great stepping stones on which to discover the beauty of each other and the expression of unconditional love.

When I reflect on my expectations and the dreams I had for my marriage, is it everything I imagined it to be?

In all fairness to my husband and I, there are moments of wedded bliss and in the beginning; there was a lot of nurturing and neediness. Occasionally, there were tantrums. New boundaries were set. Different aspects of each other emerged; some made our marriage more than I ever imagined it to be. There were moments when I felt like I could fly higher than an eagle with this man by my side (sounds cliché but it's the truth.) Then there was the downtime, the times when I wanted to scream and run, or the times when I felt so alone, even when we were both in the same room.

There were moments when my anger and frustration could easily turn me into a psychopath and it was in those moments when I asked myself, "what was I thinking when I agreed to marry this man and commit the rest of my life to this relationship?"

Lucky for me, those moments don't happen too often and even when they do, I take a step back and just witness the madness I am experiencing and recognize there is a lesson to be learned.

I liken the union of marriage to giving birth to a new baby and it going through the different stages of development.

It is a union created from love (like a baby created from love.)

Marriages/partnerships are not just an avenue to share our lives with someone we love; relationships are also a wonderful forum for personal growth. Marriage can help us discover the best and worst of each other and it can teach us what true unconditional love really is and how to express that love.

When the stars are in alignment and the chemistry is right, people are drawn together, creating a bubble of love. In this love, we see the beauty in each other, we recognize the aspects of ourselves, and we long for in the other person. It might be a nurturing nature or a strength of character we admire. In this bubble of love, we don't see the faults, we don't see the aspects that press our buttons and if we do, we tend to ignore them. We don't see the parts of ourselves that need to be healed, which are the very reason why we attract a certain person.

So while we are in this chemistry-driven bubble of love, we imagine life with this person will be wonderful and everything we ever wanted. We commit to hopefully a lifetime together. The time comes and we begin our lives together and slowly, without our awareness, the bubble begins to deflate and we start to get plugged into the reality of the relationship. He/she does something that causes us to fly off the handle, or to show a side of ourselves that we hadn't expressed before. We may start to form strong opinions about each other, their family and friends that we hadn't shared before.

We start to realize that it is one thing to be in love with this person and another to live with them. Then, we might decide to bring children into the mix and once again the dynamics change. But we soldier on, because we all seem to get so caught up in the demands of life and raising our children that we forget to live and pay attention to the relationship that we started off with, where we once had a lot of fun, when the only thing that mattered to each other was the other person and what we could do to contribute to their happiness, because this is what made us happy. So what happened? What changed?

Yes, marriage is a challenge and it will stretch us in ways we could never imagine, it can take us up and it can tear us down. There are many physical and emotional changes that happen to both men and women, such as becoming parents, menopause, job changes, the loss of a loved one, etc. All these things can have a major impact on our wellbeing.

If we are not aware of these changes, they can be misinterpreted as "my partner doesn't understand me; he/she is not supportive; we just can't seem to get along," and these assumptions may not be true. There was a time when you could share anything with this person and were once deeply in love with this person. It was a love we believed enough in that we committed our life to it. So this love must be real and alive, well at least that's what I believed and still do. At times, I think it gets covered over with the stuff of life and appears to be lost. That's when I would say, "Stop what you're doing and look a little deeper."

One question that I ask myself constantly in my marriage is, "Do I believe in the love that brought my husband and I together and is there still enough love here to do the work to revive and reconnect the relationship?" All love wants from us is that we check in from time to time and that we allow this love to work through us to express itself.

All we need is a spark and a willingness to make some effort and remember what we once felt the rest takes care of itself.

How do I know this? Because the times when my relationship didn't look that great and before I ran out the door into "The grass always seems greener somewhere else," I would pause and in that pause, I remember the love that brought us together in the first place and I question whether I could still connect with the love I had then? Were the qualities I fell in love with still there? Could my husband still make my heart skip a beat? Did he still have what it took to make me laugh? And did I still have the qualities that he fell in love with? Have we given each other the space to grow and mature? Did we still like each other? Did I still believe in this love and did I trust it to guide us back to each other?

For me, the answer was "yes," and when I shared this with my husband, he felt the same, we had just got lost in the roles, we played the husband/wife, the parents, the daughter-in-law/the son-in-law, etc.

I'm sure you get my drift and don't kid yourself. These roles, if not kept in check, can take over and consume us so that we forget who we were when we first fell in love with each other. Everything seems to be more important than each other. What I started to realize, as our children were growing up and spending less time with us, was that very soon it would be him and me and I didn't want to be sitting next someone I no longer had a connection with, simply because we didn't make the effort to look after each other and the love that brought us together. Every time we reconnect, we take our love to another level, peel off another layer and allow love to teach us about unconditional love.

It might feel a little awkward at first, especially if it is been a while since you both connected with each other, but it is not impossible.

It is really not that hard to do. Especially with today's technology, it can be as simple as sending a surprise text message or booking in a special dinner date, taking a genuine interest in each other's day, leaving notes for each other with favourite quotes. Look back at things you did before marriage and kids that gave you a lot of fun and laughter: watch a good comedy movie together, laughter is great for the soul.

Effort doesn't have to be big or expensive, it just has to have a heart that wants to share and receive love. Don't wait for your partner to make the first move; be bold and brave and get the ball rolling and believe in the love that started it all. Magic does happen.

If it seems too difficult to start, get professional help to get you started, and then go from there. So, before you decide that maybe you would be better off out of your relationship, pause. That pause may just save you and your partner a lot of heartache.

Marriage, partnerships, whatever you like to call it, requires work. Just like children need love and attention to grow and mature and like a garden needs to be watered, fed and weeded in order to sprout beautiful fruit, veggies or flowers, relationships require continual work. Without constant attention and nurturing, our children don't blossom and our gardens don't grow.

Our relationships are the same way, without constant attention and nurturing they become overgrown with unreasonable demands, clutter and a lot of weeds. When this happens, we start to lose interest in each other. We give in to the overgrowth and turn on each other. Both parties look for someone or somewhere to lay blame. We forget the commitment we made to each other in the beginning.

We forgot about the love that united us.

I believe that we are all expressions of love and our relationships are the vehicles where we learn how to express this love (our true selves.) When we experience conflict or challenges in our relationships, this love is out of alignment.

Love itself is far more intelligent than we think and it continually looks for ways to realign itself; and it doesn't always happen in blissful ways.

Challenges and conflict in our relationships don't always have to be argued out or even sorted out verbally, at times all it takes is the awareness that love is out of alignment and, at this moment, we don't know how to realign it. Then ask love itself to show you the way. This is where silence can be very helpful, to allow the love to realign itself. I'm not talking about silence that we sometimes use to withdraw from our partner, what I am referring to is to surrender that, in this moment, you don't know how to fix this. Sometimes love requires space, not dialogue, to sort itself out.

Our part is to trust the intelligence of this love to do what needs to be done. After all, it was this love that united us and I'm certain it did so with a plan, we just need to get out of way and allow this plan to unfold.

I believe life is too short to sweat the small stuff and live in a miserable marriage because we might be too proud or don't know how to bring back the spark. The spark is never lost, just buried, so get yourself some tools (creative ideas) and dig up the dirt and plant some new seeds; have some fun along the way; be daring and adventurous. Great love is worth the effort. I guarantee the effort will sprout beautiful flowers. Change doesn't happen overnight, but it does happen. Is your relationship worth the effort? I know mine was.

God bless.

Chapter 11
Parenting

Parenting also became a great avenue of self-discovery that was literally forced upon us when we had children, whether we liked it or not. Being a parent is supposed be one of the greatest experiences we can ever have and a lot of the times it is. The other times, it's not so great, it is challenging, frightening, stressful and not enjoyable at all and doesn't look anything like we imagined it to be.

For me, it became one of the greatest playgrounds of learning. I say playgrounds because at times that's what it felt like. There were plenty of new things to try, old things to try again and new ways to use them. Sometimes I had fun, sometimes I would fall and hurt myself and other times I had to think before I did anything.

I will give you a look into the playground of my parenting life to when I first discovered my husband and I were having a baby.

We hadn't been married long, 8 weeks to be exact and I had just lost my father tragically to a road accident, so I could say that the timing wasn't the best, as I found it very difficult to focus on being pregnant when I was so consumed with grief.

However, the body is a very intelligent machine and knows exactly how to do what needs to be done when everything seems out of alignment. Very naturally, it let me know that the timing wasn't right for this being to come into the world, so the body took matters into its own hands and the pregnancy was terminated. So our first experience of parenting was grief, emptiness and helplessness. I wasn't really sure what I felt, yet somehow I found a way to move on. Fortunately, a few months later we were blessed with another pregnancy. This time, I felt stronger and was in a better space and thought I was better prepared (who was I kidding? I wasn't prepared for all the physical and emotional changes to my body!) I had some illusion that I would blossom and look and feel beautiful. Yeah, right, most of the time I felt like a beached whale who craved sugar all the time. I felt sensitive to everything and was driven by my emotions.

Before I knew it, the nine months was up, it was time for our little boy to come into the world.

His delivery didn't come easy and I ended up have an emergency caesarean, so I didn't get to see him for a while.

Despite my drowsy state at the time, I am still able to recall this moment of seeing our little boy for the first time.

He was beautiful, with big, dark brown; almond shaped eyes; a mop of dark brown hair; and a personality that wanted to be noticed. He had an amazing set of lungs.

So now we were parents! Here we were with a new addition to our family. What next?

Suddenly, we were responsible for a little life and we had no skills and no idea what to do. This is one of those jobs you learn by trial and error and there is a lot of error!

I tried to breast feed and it just wouldn't work. There were more tears than milk and after many unsuccessful attempts and a day of baby blues, I gave in and went to bottle-feeding.

That brought with it feelings of guilt and inadequacy, so I didn't feel like I was off to a great start.

When the time came to take our baby home, it was 42 degrees Celsius, hot, humid and stifling. How do I keep this baby cool? Do I wrap him? Do I leave him in light clothing? I really didn't know what was best. I felt so alone and scared.

What if I can't do this? As quick as I had the thought, I suppressed it, not allowing myself to feel anything. I just got on with the task of parenting. Our baby was not a good sleeper. When I left the hospital, the nurse told me, "give him a few days, he will settle."

A few days later, a friend said, "'No, they take a couple of weeks."

I soon discovered everyone had an opinion, all different and all so sure they were right. And maybe they were, for their baby. I think I listened to everyone and ran myself ragged trying all the different things that everyone was suggesting, some from people who had never had children.

In Search of my Soul

Did my son ever settle? How could he, when I was never settled? Parenting was bloody hard work! It certainly wasn't the blissful picture I thought it would be. This was another situation in my life where I had no idea what to do and no faith in myself to do what came naturally.

I was one of seven siblings, four of which were younger than me, so it's not that I was never exposed to children; and in my upbringing, we raised each other.

A couple years later, we had our second baby: a beautiful little girl. She had the most beautiful bright pink lips and the cutest little face. Again, many were willing to give me more advice. "Oh, a second child is easier." I wonder whose child they were talking about, because it certainly wasn't mine.

The first few months were a breeze. She settled well, slept peacefully and our son adjusted very well to sharing his life with our new addition. All was good; I felt so blessed to have such an easy baby.

I certainly enjoyed it while it lasted! because it didn't last long, four months to be exact. Then she found her voice.

Some girls find it early! Life as a parent suddenly became a challenge, even greater than our first experience of parenthood.

My husband and I tried many ways to pacify our little girl. I spent many days in tracksuits and tears, trying to be the best parent I could be for our children.

No one told me that there is a qualifying period for parenting. That is what it felt like. If we could get through this time (which lasted for a few years), we could get through anything our kids threw at us. When the going gets tough, the tough get going and my husband and I pulled together to support each other through this period of parenting. It was a test of patience and endurance.

Fortunately, this experience with our daughter did bring us all closer together as a family and it also helped us make the decision that our family was complete and there would be no more children.

Our children become our greatest teachers, encouraging us through their behaviour to look at our own.

They will make us question our own upbringing and whether or not the methods our parents used to raise us would work on our children.

They teach us to be very present in the moment and learn to listen, even when we don't like what we're hearing.

Now, you can bury your head in the sand as a parent, but you will bear the consequences later down the track, or you can be aware of what is needed to raise children.

Our children need guidance, love and boundaries. They need guidance because they don't always know the way.

They need love because nothing grows without it. They need boundaries to keep them within a safe parameter to take risks as they grow and explore the world around them.

While it is wonderful to have a great relationship with our children, they don't need us to be their friends. They usually have more friends than they need. They need us to be their parents. It is a huge responsibility to have and raise children and it should not be taken lightly.

They also do not need parents pulling in different directions.

They need parents who are on the same page, who both have one agenda and that are doing what is best for the child/teenager, even if it interferes with what we want for ourselves.

We support, encourage, love and dish out discipline when it's called for. Unless we do this with confidence, our children begin to doubt us as parents, which then can create an imbalance of power.

It is when there is this imbalance that children can become more difficult to deal with, because we doubt our ability to guide them or give them sound advice when they need it.

I know we don't want to upset them. Tiptoeing around children does not work. What I have found that works is becoming aware of the different stages of my children's/teenagers development. I get to know my children and accept that they have their own personalities and what works for one child/teenager may not work for the other.

Always be honest with your children/teenager. Be very clear about what you will or won't tolerate and what your family values are, then honour and live by those values yourself, so you can lead by example.

Be aware that you do not try to live your lost dreams through your children. Encourage them to create their own dreams and then support them to achieve those dreams.

Through the process of having our own children, we can gain some understanding of our own parents and their reason for doing what they did in raising us. Different generations have different views on parenting and what worked in our parents' days may not work now. I have also discovered through having my own children that I have been able to heal a lot of my own childhood pain through the process of parenting. Be aware that you don't use children and parenting as a way of proving something to your parents, or as a pawn in a marriage break-up. Again, children are an extension of the love that brought us together with our partner. Just like when there is conflict in our relationship with our partner, love is trying to draw our attention to what needs to be healed or restored to realign that love.

The same thing happens when we are raising our children. Difficulties or conflict means this love is out of alignment and we need to look deeper than what appears on the surface. Maybe you are not really listening when the child is speaking to you. Children are very perceptive and can pick up on this. Sometimes you will need to pay attention to body language, it can say more than the spoken word.

Be aware that silence in children doesn't always mean they are well behaved, or that disruptive behaviour is a child being naughty, take a closer look.

Children need to know you've got their back and they have a safe place to fall; that, as their parents, we will be there to pick them up when and if they do fall and be there to celebrate their achievements.

Loving our children doesn't mean that we will always like what they do or how they think and view the world. They come through us but they don't belong to us.

However you choose to parent your children, know there is no right or wrong way; and you might have to change the goalposts along the way. However, if you have a heart that is full of love and an intention to do what's best for your child's greater good, even when it feels tough to deliver, then whatever happens, you have done your best as a parent.

Don't spend time dwelling on what you should have done differently; look at where you and your children stand now and make a conscious decision to do things differently.

Let your children know that you want things to be different, then set out to do what needs to be done. If you are not sure what to do differently, then seek help and learn some new skills, or talk to other parents. There are also a lot of great books, written by knowledgeable people that can offer good advice.

Our children are a gift and my husband and I feel blessed to have them in our life, so we will always strive to be the best that we can be as parents and not take our responsibility lightly. Remember to laugh; God knows there's a lot to laugh about as we all find our way through the maze of parenting.

If you plant good seeds, you will reap good fruit. Have faith in yourself and a heart full of love and you'll be surprised how it all turns out. Through my children, I am reminded to lighten up and laugh at myself. We are raising the next generation: what sort of a future would you like to see?

On the humorous side of parenting, be good to your children: they may well decide which nursing home you go to.

God bless

Chapter 12
Our Beautiful Bodies.

Our body is a source of constant torment, not because that's what bodies do, but because of our perception and expectation of our bodies. Learning to listen to my body was a great challenge because so much of how I saw myself was wrapped up in my body image.

When we were born, we came in a physical body simply because there is no other way to be human, so our body is a great necessity that served us well as a child. For without our bodies, there would be nothing to carry our spirit.

Bodies come in all shapes and sizes, it is never one-size-suits-all and can you imagine how it would be if we all looked alike.

I believe there are reasons why we come in a certain shape and size and I believe it has a lot to do with what we are here to learn and understand about ourselves.

This body carries us around in our daily lives. It allows us to experience many different things because, as human beings, there is no other way to have these experiences.

Our bodies allow us to move in so many ways, such as walking, running, skipping, dancing, driving cars, riding bikes, etc. The body has a great system that digests the food we feed it in order to sustain our lives and eliminate what it doesn't need on a daily basis.

In this body, we can talk, think, feel, hear, see, taste, flaunt and flirt. We can laugh and cry, express love and anger, dress it in beautiful clothing and achieve amazing challenges. You name it, if we are brave and willing, we could probably do it. We are so blessed to be able to do so many things in this body that we have been given.

You do believe that, don't you?

Think about animals for a minute. They can't do all the things with their bodies that we can and given the way animals live, they have no need to use their bodies the way humans do. So, therefore, we are blessed, aren't we?

If we really did believe that we are blessed to have the body we have, then why are so many hell-bent on self destruction of their bodies? Why do we do so many horrible things to our bodies?

Most of us wouldn't treat our best friends they way we treat our bodies, but we don't think twice about what we do to ourselves. We flog it with exercise; we run it ragged with endless jobs.

We twist and turn it, pushing it harder and harder. Exercise is very good for us, but it doesn't have to be extreme all the time. Work is also good for us, but we need to remember to come up for air occasionally and share the load whenever we can.

We keep our bodies up until all hours of the night, then struggle to get out of bed in the morning.

Late nights in small doses are fine; however, sleep is where we get to rest and restore our bodies.

We have plastic surgery to lift this part, drop that part, add this, remove that, we Botox our faces so that we show no emotion, desperately trying to hang on to youth, believing that wrinkles are somehow shameful and aging is illegal.

I once heard someone say, "The wrinkles on my face tell a story of the life I have lived," and we never know when that story may need to be told.

We put ourselves through endless diets, on today, off tomorrow and feed our body so much garbage—whatever is easy and quick, or we starve it to death in pursuit of the perfect body. I have yet to find the perfect body, given that everyone has a different perception of what constitutes beauty and perfection. After all, beauty is in the eye of the beholder. We numb our bodies with drugs and alcohol because it's easier than having to feel our emotions.

Doctors tell people that red wine is good for you, so they build themselves a cellar to store their wine collection.

Most of the things I grew up with that were once a luxury are now in abundance and affordable, so there's no need for discipline.

Some choose to pierce their bodies with all these odd bits of metal, or use it as a canvas and tattoo all kinds of things onto it. Don't get me wrong, a tattoo here or there can look interesting and piercings in appropriate places (ears) can look great.

It's just that sometimes art looks better in a frame or on a wall. At least it can be taken down when it becomes boring to look at and replaced with something new.

Some of those metal pieces might be put to better use in a car motor or machinery. In all fairness to those who have piercings, you do have the option of removing them when the novelty wears off.

I'm not saying that all these things we do to our bodies are bad and I'll be the first to say I've had my fair share of bodily destruction and I have plenty of scars to remind me of it.

If only I had the wisdom I have now back then, though it could be argued that it was through the self-destruction that I learned the wisdom.

We torture and taunt our bodies, never giving ourselves permission to just be in our bodies the way they are.

We can try and run from the body we have and we might experience moments when we achieve the look we want, but it's fleeting. The reason most of us can't sustain those moments is because the body needs to change from the inside, not the outside.

It works like this: clean up the distortion and the disillusion you feel inside yourself and the outside will naturally shine.

How often do we see some achieve their goal weight by strenuous methods, but their happiness doesn't last and it's not long before all the weight is put back on?

Are all those who have body piercings happy, or all those who have used their bodies as a canvas to paint on, are they happy? What about those who drink? It's one thing to celebrate a joyous occasion; it's another to drink daily. Is that happiness? Drugs? well, that speaks for itself: if you were happy, then the last thing you'd want to do is numb yourself.

Until we can make peace with our bodies, until we can look out ourselves in a mirror and say "I love you just the way you are, warts and all; we will never be at peace in our own skin. Living with an eating disorder for many years and constantly wanting my body to look different so that I could feel better about myself was a good indicator of the loathing I had for my body. I'm sure there are many out there reading this who know exactly what it feels like to live like this. It took a lot of work and commitment to change my perception of myself and after all these years, I have finally reached a place in my body where it is peaceful and I have accepted the body I have been given. It's not picture perfect and I have stopped trying to achieve that.

I have learned to honour this body and look after it, so hopefully it will go the distance into old age, without illness or disease. I've stopped fighting with my mind that kept telling me I needed to look this way or that way. I am learning more and more to listen to my body's needs.

I believe our body carries our spirit. However, if we continually abuse our body, we don't give our spirit the opportunity to shine and to guide us. Our body is incredibly resilient, no matter what we throw at it and throw into it, somehow it bounces back.

But I wonder if our body's resilience is running out, have we pushed too hard? Do we really think it only happens to others? We just have to look the statistics on cancer, heart disease, strokes, diabetes, etc, to know something's not working anymore. These diseases don't discriminate, they are not racist: any age, any color, just go for a walk in some of our hospitals and you will know what I'm talking about. Illnesses are starting in younger bodies at a very fast rate.

I, for one, was diagnosed with gallstones at fifteen years old, which was unheard of thirty-five years ago.

Not a day goes by that someone doesn't mention someone who has just been diagnosed with some disease or someone who just passed away from an illness.

What is it? The food we consume, attitude, genetics, lifestyle, ignorance, maybe a combination of all these things?

Maybe it's none of these and it's just bad luck, who really knows?

Let's just take a stab in the dark here. Let's say that it's the food we are eating. Look at what you eat: is it fresh and natural? How much of it is fresh fruit for sugar to sweeten the body, wholesome vegetables for nourishment and fibre to cleanse the body, whole grains, seeds, or nuts? All these things come from nature and were put here to feed us, untouched by human hands. Humans are an act of nature, so why would we want to feed our bodies anything other than what nature intended?

Look at animals, they survive and thrive on the abundance of nature. We don't see them in fast food stores or eating genetically modified food.

Then let's look at attitude: if we are able to respect and honour ourselves and take better care of ourselves, I believe we would be in a better place to take care of and generate a community spirit. When we give to others, we thrive and it makes us feel good and useful. We then would change attitudes and become more tolerant human beings, appreciating ourselves and the goodness of our generous spirit, giving us a sense of peace and fulfillment.

Genetics, well there is not a lot we can do about that, other than become aware of what runs through our families, then do our best to live in ways that don't enhance those things.

What about lifestyle: if we were able to simplify our lives, need less things, rest more, share more, and create a community spirit and help each other, ask for help when we need it, we would be more relaxed; less stressed and have more time for some fun and laughter, which would be great for our bodies. Laughter is known as a great healing medicine and doesn't cost a cent. No amount of money can buy the joy that a good belly laugh can give us.

Life is about balance and it is through our body that we live out that balance. Everything in moderation: even our thoughts need to be in moderation, so when you become aware that your mind is making unrealistic demands on your body, then you pull back, pause for a moment and think about the consequences of not listening to your body's needs.

Do any of us stop to think of the impact and how many lives are affected when we get sick or when we are so stressed we lose sight of how to treat others, let alone ourselves?

I am aware that people need to work and bills need to be paid and families need to be fed, but it doesn't have to be that hard.

When my husband and I lost our home because we could no longer afford to keep it and my husband was on centrelink payments because his work was seasonal, we managed because we simplified our lives. We sorted out ways that made life easier so we could take care of our family.

We focused on creating a balance in our life without the stress and somehow the universe always provided.

So take a good, hard and long look at your perception of your body and how you are treating it. Think about how you want your body to carry you through your life and if you recognize that you are on a path of self-destruction, try looking at it as a wake-up call, that something in your life needs your attention. If you get sick your body is screaming out to you to change things, to listen to what it needs and trust what your body, not your mind, is trying to tell you.

You only get one body in this life, here and now. Don't wait until it's too late to do something differently and if you don't know where to start, find someone who can guide you. There are a lot of skilled people out there with the experience and knowledge to teach you.

It has been through my body that I have learned a lot about my spirit and how to live a fulfilling life; and it is

In Search of my Soul

never too late to change the body. Cells continually renew themselves and our bodies know how to heal themselves; you do your part and trust your body to do its part.

Make your life count, because you are worth it and you can't do that without a body.

It's your call.

God bless

Chapter 13
Money

Money is a commodity that also taught me a lot about myself and how I viewed and used it and again life was never short of experiences to learn these lessons.

Money, by definition in the dictionary, means "pieces of metal or certificates used to buy and sell."

"Money, money, money must be funny in a rich man's world!"

Great lyrics for a song, but in reality do you think it would be fun in a rich man's world?

Money means different things to different people, not everyone sees it or uses it in their lives in the same way.

Money is used to control people, to manipulate others, to help others, to hurt people and mostly it is used for what it is meant for: to help us sustain a livable existence.

Let's take a closer look at what money is. I will share with you my perception of money. I believe money is an energy, it is a tool given to us to use in our life to provide shelter, food, education, medical care, etc.

Money is a commodity that needs to be earned, something that most people work for.

In bygone years, people would trade things in exchange for food or shelter. This was known as bartering and I'm sure there are still people in places around the world who use this system and it seems to work well.

Money is made to go around and continually circulate. Money generates financial wealth for some people and burns a hole in the pockets of others.

Money can provide some with an abundance of material possessions, while leaving others with nothing but the clothes on their back.

Money can give people the opportunity to experience many wonderful things in their lives, such as travelling to beautiful and exciting place around the world, or doing things that they may never have been able to do if they weren't financially wealthy.

Some would say, "Money is the root of all evil" I guess if you believe this statement to be true, then that is how money will manifest for you in your life.

Personally, I don't believe this statement to be true. I believe it is one's perception of money and how it is used that creates the evil, not money itself.

Money is just money--a piece of paper or bits of metal. It does not have evil printed all over it. But put it in the hands of some people and watch evil manifest!

Why do some people have more money than others, almost like they have magnet fingers that money just sticks to, or a tree in their backyard that keeps producing an abundance of money on call?

Then there are some that no matter how much they work or try to save, money just slips through their fingers and they always seem to run short.

Then there are others who seem to think, "If I could just hit the jackpot in the lottery, or pick the winning horse, or the next shot at the poker machine, I'll be set for life," only to end up worse off than when they started.

Money, money, money, so much of our lives revolves around money; whether we like it or not, for better or worse, it is here to stay.

Why is it that some struggle more than others with money?

I think there are a number of reasons for this, some are very clear and others leave us wondering!

The ones that are clear are that some people worker harder than others, they may be in higher-paid jobs, or have good financial advice guiding them to make good profitable investments, or they have a wise perception of money and how to use it.

Some inherit large sums of money from wealthy relatives.

While for some, this is a blessing and can be a great help, especially if one is struggling to make ends meet. For others, it can create a living hell. How many families have been ripped to shreds because of inheritance?

Others have strong beliefs about money and believe they deserve and will always have, money and the universe provides in abundance.

Then there are those who never seem to make ends meet, going from one struggle to another. Why is that?

Maybe these people are in low-paying jobs, or living above their means. They play the part of two-bob millionaires.

They may not know how to manage their money.

What about their beliefs about money? It might be that these people believe they don't deserve money, or that there is never enough money to make ends meet, or that they need to work hard for money.

And then we have those who believe that the government owes them an income and should provide for them, so they decide not to work and just live off of welfare.

Regardless of whether we are financially wealthy or not, both sides of the spectrum are learning experiences. Our perceptions of money and the karma it creates will determine what our experiences and lessons are for each individual.

How we use and view money can bring out a generous spirit of giving. We can help those less fortunate and provide food and shelter for those who may not have the ability, for whatever reason, to provide that for themselves. Many financially wealthy people donate large amounts of money to many charities. Some make it known and others do it discreetly and there are many generous people making a big difference in the lives of others through their generosity.

In others, it might bring forward a selfish perception, believing that it is not their responsibility to help or provide for others and it's every man for himself.

For some, the way they view and use money brings forward greed, whereby no matter how much money they have, they just want more and more and will do anything to get it.

There are people who also believe having money is a way of validating their sense of self. If they have plenty, then they see themselves as superior or more worthy than those less fortunate and then those that believe that, because they don't have money, they are not worthy.

Each one of these experiences will be filled with the grace of learning. Without experience, it is difficult to learn.

There was a time in my life where I worked 3 jobs, believing I had to work really hard to earn money. I learned that, while it is great to have a good work ethic, it was not going to make me wealthier. For me, it was about learning how to use my money that made a difference. In my married life, for my husband and me, it was through our personal experiences of loss that our perception of money was again challenged. So, when we lost our home and we were forced to rent and my husband was on welfare due to his work being seasonal, we learned through those experiences that our lives are not controlled by money and we will always have enough. We got through this time in our lives stress-free, learning more skills about money management and that a simple life can bring a lot of joy. We were never deprived and lived quite well with what we had.

I recall that, one Sunday afternoon my husband said to me that he wanted to go into his workplace to see if there was anything available. He said that he only had five dollars in his pocket and wasn't sure he should go. I suggested that he go anyway and just see what happens and not focus on money and just have faith that all would be well. He went that night, as his workplace was night work. He was given work for the night, bringing home eighty-five dollars and two days later was offered work until his season started.

This meant we could come off of welfare and he could provide for his family, all because he took a leap of faith.

We have never looked back. Losing our house was a great blessing and many lessons were learned because of the experience. In our life, money is a commodity that we use to provide for the things we need to make our life comfortable.

I believe that all our needs will be provided for and the money will always be there. We live our lives with gratitude. All that comes our way is received with thanks, appreciation and gratitude.

Many choose to worship money and make it more important than anything else; when this happens, one is never able to truly enjoy the fruits of their labour, watching everything with hawk eyes. Everything in their lives revolves around money. It is one thing to be frugal and another to be stingy. Frugal teaches you to get the best out of what you have and stingy stops you from enjoying what you've got. Families are torn apart because of money being made more important than relationships. Some people give money so much power that they allow it to control their lives, forsaking everything else, yet many wealthy people have experienced that, in the face of death, no amount of money can save you. Money can't buy you life. It may give you opportunities to try different methods of treatments, but it will not save you from death. I'm sure, when our time comes and we are faced with death, how many of us will focus on money? How many will lie there counting the money they made or have accumulated over the years? Don't you think, at that moment, it's the people who surround you, the love that you have had and given in your life that will be at the forefront? Wouldn't you want to think you were worth more than your bank account that your life had more substance than that?

And if it's not, then I think you might want to take a good look at your perception of money.

So, back to the original question, is it fun in a rich man's world? It's all about perception. While money can't buy happiness, there are many benefits to being financially wealthy, but it's not to say that life can't be just as rewarding without an abundance of money.

God bless

CHAPTER 14
The Blessing of Life

Life, right from the beginning, the very moment of conception, is a miracle.

It always is, has been and always will be the most amazing miracle of creation.

Isn't it amazing that, from a tiny little sperm and a little egg, so many lives are created? All are individuals and every one of them is unique in their own way. In no other form other than that of a human being are we able to experience love and explore life. Life always brings something different into the world and all of us bring something into the lives of each other.

Life itself constituted the most exciting lessons I learned on this journey. Not just lessons about my life, but the lives and greatness of others.

Lucy Pignataro

So many wonderful gifts come to the world through the lives that are created. Every time a baby is born, life is showing us its best work and the miracle of life.

Never underestimate that miracle called life and the lessons and gifts that come with it.

So many talents, amazing inspiration, so much love; all these gifts serve a purpose for all our lives.

Wonderful musicians bring the gift of beautiful music that inspires others to bring forth their own voices and music, writers share their gift of knowledge and wisdom and write great books and poetry that spreads and empowers the lives of many, great athletes motivate us to aspire to our own physical strengths, creative artists put beautiful art on canvas or mold incredible statues.

We have people with a great ability to lead and guide others; wonderful men and women using their lives to serve our countries and communities.

Heroic fireman, policemen, doctors and nurses put the safety of others before their own.

We have builders, plumbers, and concreters, all offering great skills to build our homes, shopping centre's and businesses.

I have given you just a few examples of great gifts that most of us would think of, but what about the wonderful creations we don't often think about?

I'm talking about the lives that come to this world with disabilities and the gifts they bring to the rest of us.

They bring with them gifts of compassion, empathy, unconditional love and patience, teaching us the importance of accepting differences. All of which are such an important necessity if we are to live together in peace and harmony.

Even those lives that are very short-lived and their bodies are used for science to find cures for the rest of us are worth something. No life is for nothing.

No life comes without a purpose, good, bad, beautiful, or ugly, long-term or short, all teaching, evolving and aspiring to live their own life.

Even prisoners bring the gift of the importance of discipline, rules and boundaries, for without them everyone would run around in a mad frenzy, wreaking havoc.

Everyone one of us serves a purpose on this earth; we are not mistakes! Some of us may have come by accident, or so we are told, but I'm not sure that I buy that, as I believe everything is as it should be in any given moment.

Every human life has been created with a task in mind.

Our job is to discover what that task is that can best express our gift or gifts and then serve through that task, bringing forward our own unique gift to the world.

It is my belief that no task or gift is greater or lesser than another; they're just tasks that bring different gifts forward.

As we can all see, it takes many different roles and services to keep the world going, to make this planet what it is.

Some roles are more glorified than others. That glorification is only our perception and doesn't place any importance on these roles, even though many would say that there is that importance. There are many roles that offer a lot more money for different gifts, but even that doesn't make the role greater.

Yes, there are roles that carry greater responsibilities with them and again, the people in those roles obviously have the gift best suited to those roles.

I believe the fact that we each learn and deliver information in our own unique way has a big part to play in the tasks we are gifted to deliver.

The garbologist's task, for instance, is just as great and important as a brain surgeon's.

A surgeon is gifted with a brain to absorb complex information, and then use that information to save lives, whereas a garbologist is gifted with the physical strength to remove rubbish from suburbs. It is amazing minds that come up with ways to use our rubbish in recycling plants, creating new things out of old ones.

What would the world be like if we didn't have people who specialize in getting rid of our rubbish?

Where would we be without our amazing surgeons and doctors that save lives every day? They study so hard to find cures for diseases and illnesses.

Everywhere we look around in our daily lives, someone is performing a task that can serve others.

The girl in the supermarket offers her time to serve us, so we can do our grocery shopping and feed our families.

The guy at the service station is there putting petrol/gas in our cars so we can run them and get around in our daily lives.

The street sweeper keeps our streets clean, the wonderful nurses in our hospitals and nursing homes serving the sick, frail and old. Scientists test and experiment on new ways to live, or new medicines for better health.

Millions of women serve by raising children.

What about all the great actors/actresses and comedians who keep us entertained?

The list goes on and on; I am sure there are tasks I can't even name. This list is endless.

All these task and roles are avenues for all of us to perform and express our gifts, whatever they might be and sometimes, through these tasks/roles, new ones are created, further expanding the avenue to express the great gifts of life.

Take the time to think about the many different tasks that you know of think of your own and ask yourself, "how do

I feel about the task I perform and is it delivering my gift to the world? Do I see the greatness in myself and the gifts I bring forward?"

Do you value your gifts and the life you were given to deliver these gifts?

So many don't value the life and gifts they were given and continually compare themselves to others, measuring their worth by the task they perform, believing that someone else's task has greater value than their own.

When we measure our worth by other people's gifts, we will always be disappointed. We are who we are, no lesser or greater than anyone else. We are all here to learn and grow and we may not all have to learn the same lessons, but make no mistake; we are here to make a difference. It is our perception of ourselves and our gifts that makes us feel less than we are.

I believe in every life lies the opportunity for growth of the human spirit. The tasks that we perform are an avenue to explore our gifts. At times, we perform tasks that don't reveal our gifts, yet those are a path that leads to exploration of those gifts. At times, many give up before they have had a chance to discover their gifts and their place in the world.

I will be the first to say that, while some know from a very young age what they are gifted with and how to bring that gift forward into the world to serve others, some of us and I include myself, had no idea and have performed many different tasks in search of our gift.

When I finally discovered my gift, I was surprised to find it was always present in my life and I was using it in service natural. The difference between how I use it now is that I now give it a name: as a Life Coach and Counselor and this gift continues to reveal other gifts. So, I like to call myself a work in progress.

I have always had a natural ability to guide people, listen to their troubles and offer them comfort, empathy and support.

If you look closely at your life, what natural gift do you have?

Most of the time, our gifts are staring us in the face; we are just too distracted by looking at others to see our own.

We don't have to climb mountains or take endless courses to discover our gifts.

In Search of my Soul

However, in saying that, sometimes we need to take courses to refine our gift, or to strengthen our confidence to express our gift. What do you do that lights you up that makes you happy whenever you are doing a particular thing?

Trust me, it is there you just need to look a little closer.

If you can't see it, then try this: what do you imagine yourself doing that makes you smile, what's the gift in what you see and do you already have that, or is fear blocking the gift?

At times, we are so afraid of being judged by others that we don't allow our gifts to shine; we keep them well hidden, even from ourselves. This is where I would say to you: "Feel the fear and do it anyway.' Be bold, be brave, your gift could make a great difference in the world and you will never know what that difference will be until you put it out there. The other thing is when we finally let our gifts shine through; we live fulfilled lives and just keep going from strength to strength. Just being brave enough to put it out will inspire others to do the same. There is nothing worse than living life feeling like we don't belong or can't contribute.

Don't live with "what if?' Don't get to the end of your life and when you look back, say, "I wish I had done this" or "I wish I had tried that," go on, have a go the time is now. As I said before, we are not here by accident; there are no mistakes. We are here to serve, learn and grow.

So many are sitting around believing they weren't gifted with anything and do very little to contribute to life. They are living unfulfilled lives.

Even if we only ever change one other person's life, we have made a difference. We have used our gift. When we step into our gifts and serve, we pave the way for others to do the same.

Many continually go in search of happiness. On my journey, I have discovered happiness is living your life just the way you are, sharing the wonderful gift of your life without expectation of being someone other than yourself.

Many are unhappy because they are too busy looking in someone else's backyard, wishing it was theirs.

Look in your own backyard; you don't know what great seeds are planted there, just waiting to sprout.

Dig up the dirt and find out. You might have to pull out some weeds to get to the seeds, but that is half the fun of learning.

Don't underestimate the value of your own life and the difference you make to the lives of others.

We are all here to live our best lives, however that life presents itself.

Don't judge yourself by your looks or your level of intelligence; look inside your heart, because that's what will lead you to your gift.

A lot of the most amazing people in this world were given very little support or encouragement. In fact, many were put down and told they would never amount to anything.

It's a good thing they chose not to listen. These people have made a difference in the world today.

When we fulfill our life purpose, the beauty and the wisdom that comes from that truly make our lives worthwhile.

Whatever you do in this life, make it count and let your spirit shine. You are amazing your life is part of the miracle of life don't waste another minute. Live your best life.

God bless

Chapter 15
Meditation

What is meditation? How do you meditate? And what are the benefits of meditation? These are the questions that I asked when I was first told about meditation.

According to the dictionary, meditation means -reflect deeply on spiritual matters.

I would say it is also a technique to draw ones attention within one self with focus and awareness to bring about a state of stillness and peace.

I have been meditating for fourteen years, in this time I have learnt to draw my attention within and not get caught up in my thoughts and dialogue going on in my head. Through the consistent practice of meditation I have learnt to transcend the thoughts and dialogue to a space of peace and tranquility. Throughout my practice of meditation I have become a lot more conscious of the way I live my life. I have become aware of how I react to different situations in

In Search of my Soul

my life, and in the state of awareness I am then able to choose how I react rather than be seduced my senses and thoughts. By enabling myself to choose how to react I spare others and myself the brunt of misused emotions. Which is what happens when we react without thinking or pausing it usually doesn't turn out well, either hurting ourselves or someone else. However with awareness we have time to step back and see things clearly, thinking about the best outcome for all concerned.

I have come to realize that meditation is a great healing tool and avenue for personal growth, by surrendering to the process and trusting the intelligence of my being I am able to move through painful emotions in a way that doesn't overwhelm me. I am letting go of my emotions at a steady pace. There are also health benefits to meditation such as lowering blood pressure, calming anxiety; it has been known to help with managing depression, it is also a great way to refresh and energies, meditation can also draw your attention to anything else going on in the body that needs to be looked at and addressed. Through meditation I learnt to connect with my spirit and pay attention to inner guidance, heightening my awareness to listen and follow my truth. I believe my meditation practice has made me a better person in all areas of my life not for the purpose of acceptance by others but for my greater good. The benefits of my meditation practice has spilled out into my family life; creating a more peaceful and balanced environment, whereby we have more respect for each other and the paths we are on individually and as a whole family unit. Meditation has taught me to be more mindful of others and how I interact with them. It has been a great tool to be used when I'm feeling stressed, confused or lack direction. Meditation helps me to become grounded in my body and realign with my breath, bringing about a sense of stillness and peace; staying in this state for a while can restore and balance me so I am able to see things clearly or can give me the confidence to make decisions that may have seemed difficult initially.

It is also important to know there will be times when the most peaceful meditation can stir up a string of restless emotions which can leave me wondering why I even bothered to sit still. Trust me when this happens whilst it is uncomfortable, meditation has just created an avenue to release unnecessary baggage to restore a balance in my life.

When this happens just becoming aware of what is going on, observing without reacting and using the breath at this time till the restlessness settles.

I recall the first time I tried to meditate without knowing much about it and the process would stir up emotions and my mind would become so restless causing nothing but frustration. It wasn't until I learnt more about meditation with people who had been meditating for a long time that it became a lot more comfortable and enjoyable. Meditation has become an integral part of my life and how I live it and I couldn't imagine my life without it. Meditation has become as important as breathing. As a wife and a mother I encourage my children and husband to meditate especially in times of difficulties or when their lives become challenging. One of the things that has become more evident in our family is that we all live more fulfilled lives.

We live in such a fast paced society where no one seems to have time for anything, always running here, there, everywhere and getting nowhere, gaining nothing more than a lot of stress and anxiety. Meditation helps to stop the madness quieting the voice that keeps propelling us into fast pace action. Meditation reminds us to breath, to stop and smell the roses. Meditation is not religion based and not only for certain people, we are all capable of being still, it might start off challenging and rightly so; when we are so use to running and there's hundreds of thoughts running through our heads, it won't just stop, it takes practice over and over and over again and in time it becomes easier to be still, the noise in our head becomes quieter, the restlessness in our body settles and there you have it meditation.

Initially I would recommend that anyone thinking of taking up the practice of meditation to find a group or workshop that has guided meditations and learn from experienced meditators, this will help to give you more confidence when you set up your own practice at home, it is also good to share your meditation experiences with others. However I will say do not compare your meditation to others as we will each experience meditation in our own unique way. Comparing to others may make you feel you are doing something wrong and there is no wrong meditation.

There will be times when your commitment will be very consistent and then other times when it will fluctuate and that's fine. Over time you will come to value this time you give yourself and the benefits that come with it. If you are a parent with young children when you feel confident enough in your own practice teach your children how to be still there are many guided meditation books for children. This will help them to become more grounded and centered in themselves, meditation will also help them to trust themselves as they grow and develop. Meditation is not a new technique and has been around for thousands of years, and in many countries has never been lost, however the busy pace of western culture needs re-educating on the art of silence and being still. Once you become familiar with meditation you will wonder how you ever got by without it. Meditation is the vehicle that brings us back to who we are at the very core of our being it puts us in touch with our essence. Teaching us to trust the guidance within. Over time we will be able to identify the voice of the ego and the voice of our spirit. The more we become aware of our ego and how it plays out in our lives, the more we will be able to rise above it and respond from a more centered place aligned with our truth. Spirit will allow us to fulfill our lives with understanding, compassion, and our truth, ego with fill us with false hope and disillusion leaving us feeling empty and lost.

I hope I have inspired you to at the very least take a look at meditation a little closer and give it a try, it may turn out to be one of the best decisions you make for your health and wellbeing.

God bless

Chapter 16
Friendships

Friendships what are they? How do they impact our lives? Are they meant to last life times? Or are they for a rhyme a reason and a season? According to the dictionary friendships mean affection, affinity, alliance, amity, attachments, good- fellowship. There were many more descriptions' to many in fact to list. My interruption of a friendship is a relationship with others. That can be in many different forms, such as friendships with work colleagues these friendship may not be very intimate, and the friendship may only be shared in the workplace. Then we might have neighborly friendships, again these two may not be on a personal level, by that I mean we may have the occasional get together but not share a lot about our personal selves. Then there are friendships that we socialize with on a more regular basis, these may or may not be on a personal level. There are times when friends come into our lives for a short time, they come to help us learn lessons and once those lessons are learned the friendship dissolves and each of us moves on. Sometimes there will be friendships that happen very quickly when we are really struggling with something in our lives, these friends seem to offer the right words, comfort or nurturing needed to get us through where others can't. Then we will have a few near and dear friends that we confide in and share a lot of our personal lives with, these are the friendship we come to rely on when we are faced with life challenges, relationship breakups, job loss, or the loss of a loved one. These friendships offer us support, compassion and understanding we may face challenges together, yet there is enough love in the friendship to find ways to overcome them. They help to give us strength when we can't seem to find it in ourselves. If we are lucky these friendships last for a lifetime and the friendship supports our growth as we move through life and our life experiences. Then sometimes we need to recognize that these friendships have served their purpose and no longer fulfill or support either party so we need to let go and move on. This isn't always easy and some hang on in the hope that things will change or go back to the way it use to be. It is never easy to let go of the things in our lives that have become familiar and feel safe even if they no longer feel comfortable or serve a purpose and it can sometimes take awhile before we would even admit it to ourselves that it no longer feels right or comfortable let alone admit it to the other person. At times the other person maybe feeling the same and going through the same internal struggle and sometimes they are not even aware that things have changed. So what do we do about it?

Firstly take a moment to think about the friendships you have, and ask yourself do I still feel nurtured and supported and do I still enjoy being in this friendship? I am still being a nurturing and supportive friend? Be honest with yourself, do you feel like you have out grown this friendship and you struggle to relate? Do you come home feeling drained and exhausted after being with this friend or friends, is your friendship one sided, meaning you are making all the effort! Does your friend always make excuses as to why they didn't call or maybe you are always left waiting because they are always running late. If any of these scenarios are going on in your friendships then maybe it's time to move on. If you struggle to let go, you can try and share what you feel with your friend and openly discuss where you both sit in the relationship and see if there is a way of moving forward that would still nurture and support the friendship. If that doesn't feel right or you don't feel you can be that open and honest with your friend then ease out of the friendship slowly, call less frequently and spend less time together and the friendship will slowly dissolve making it easier to move on. Friendships are also a good barometer to recognize how much we have grown and changed over the years. Things that we once thought were of great importance in our friendship may not have much bearing anymore and things we once didn't give much thought to suddenly seems to be of importance. However unless we take the time to reflect on the friendship and think about the lessons, learning and blessings that have come to you because of this friendship or to look at where this friendship maybe holding you back, has it become comfortable, too comfortable that it keeps you safe and so you don't challenge yourself to make new friends or try something different. Are you afraid of change? And live by the saying "Better the devil you know, than the one you don't "~

You will not know whether this friendship is worth hanging on to or you need to cut the ties and move on. If I have learnt anything from life, it is that change is going to happen whether we like it or not and we can either surrender to it and go with the flow and trust the process of life or we can hang on to things whether they be jobs, friendships, relationships that no longer serve our purpose and be miserable as we struggle to stay in the same place and not grow from the experience.

I have let go of many friendships throughout my life and in the process learnt a lot about myself, others and life through those friendships. The more I learnt to love and accept myself the more I attracted people who supported and encouraged me on my life s journey. I discovered that sometimes our friends would prefer not to watch us grow and become successful or have a loving relationship and can judge us harshly when we make a decision for our greater good. Sometimes our personal growth makes our friends feel uncomfortable and they can find ways to sabotage our growth. These friendships need closer inspection. How is it serving our growth by staying in this friendship?

In Search of my Soul

Sometimes the answer isn't always clear and it might take a few attempts before there is enough courage to walk away. Not all friendships hinder our growth there are the ones that are here for a lifetime, there seems to be and ebb and a flow to these. These friendships are supportive, encouraging are fun to be in and seem effortless with both parties enjoying time together. There is no pressure to be anyone other than you. It is better to have one true friend that allows us to be ourselves than to have many unfulfilled friendships. Life will always give us many wonderful and valuable experiences to share with others. It is when we recognize the blessing and the lessons that we are able to flourish through our friendships whether we stay for a life time or a short time. No man or woman is an island and we can all use a friend.

God bless

Chapter 17
Gratitude

Gratitude, I love this word, such a beautiful word that touches the heart. Without gratitude life has no substance.

According to the dictionary Gratitude means - to be thankful, counting your blessings, noticing simply pleasures and acknowledging everything that you receive. It means learning to live your life as if everything were a miracle, and being aware on a continuous basis of how much you've been given. Gratitude shifts you from focusing on what you think your life lacks to the abundance that is steadily present.

According to Dr Emmons Gratitude increases your level of happiness, 'to say we feel grateful is not to say that everything in our lives is necessarily great. It just means we are aware of our blessings: Think about that for a minute 'to be aware of our blessings' just saying it can bring forth a sense of lightness.

For me gratitude means being thankful for everyday that I get to live life to the fullest, good or bad it is another opportunity to try again, to learn and grow and share with others on this amazing journey of life.

In Search of my Soul

I'm grateful for my health and well being, I am grateful for my family and friends, I am grateful for my home and my work and grateful for the experiences life presents me because it is only through these experiences that I am able to grow, evolve as a human being and fulfill my purpose. When I take the time every day to reflect on the abundance

I have in my life my spirit feels lighter and brighter, I face the day with more enthusiasm and joy. I look forward to participating fully and being present in my life.

Shifting our focus to being grateful can make the darkest days seem a little easier to bear.

Gratitude is like a frequency of love and can have a great affect on our being and those that are around us. We can spread it like a virus just by thinking well of others and ourselves and being grateful for the opportunity to share our life with others. Living life with gratitude is a great way to help overcome fear. When we are grateful for all that life gives us there is nothing to fear and a brave heart emerges.

Even the most challenging events or experiences carry a blessing. When we focus on gratitude we are able to acknowledge that blessing.

When I look back on my life I can see that all that came my way good, bad, ugly, frightening, I am so grateful that I was given those experiences because they taught me so much about life and my place in it, these experience also prepared me for other greater experiences that came along throughout my journey.

Had I not been able or willing to shift my focus to gratitude I believe I would have been consumed with bitterness and a lack of love for myself and others. I choose not to be defined by these experiences and look for the blessing which was always there sometimes clear and other times not so clear yet still there.

Filling your heart and mind with gratitude is like turning on a heater in an ice cold room everyone gets warm.

Take a moment and reflect over your life as it was and as it is and start to focus on being grateful for all the small things and the things you took for granted and maybe still do, as that becomes comfortable allow yourself to focus on the difficult experiences and as you do this breath gently into your body and relax, it is in this relaxed state that we can begin to see the blessings that came from these experiences? For some it may take a few attempts before it becomes clear and some things won't be clear and that's ok be gentle with yourself, just by being grateful for your wiliness to try is a good start. Make a commitment to yourself to write down five things a day that you are grateful for and slowly adding more and more things to your list. Take note of how you are feeling and how life becomes a little easier and a little clearer, relationships start to change and become more loving when we become grateful for the ones we have. Our jobs become more pleasant to be in when we are grateful for the work we do. Our days become brighter just because we are grateful to be alive. The more we practice living with gratitude the more we find to be grateful for.

It is not hard to think about and then begin to practice being grateful, it really does take little effort and the outcome is wonderful. You just have to ask people who live with gratitude everyday and you will see they are a pleasure to be around.

'Gratitude' why not give it a try and see what happens; you have nothing to lose and a lot to gain.

God bless

Chapter 18
I found my soul

After searching high and low and believing it was somehow separate from me, I finally found my soul and in finding it, I realized *it* had never left me and was never something separate from me. I had just covered it with many layers of impressions that I had gathered throughout my life that made it impossible to see what my reality was.

We have no idea just how much we absorb and are influenced by the lives of others and our upbringing.

We surrender so much of ourselves in order to gain approval, recognition, acceptance and love from others.

So many of us live lives that are stifled by the beliefs and limitations of the people who raised us, that's not to say that it was intentional on their part, it is just the way life is, each of us doing what we think is best or what we know, even if *it* is to the detriment of others. Yet, this can sometimes become the cornerstone that pushes us to go in search of the self, bringing forward greater awareness and

In Search of my Soul

self-knowledge in order to change the cycles that can be destructive and disempowering.

This chapter is the culmination of the many experiences I have had and the even greater lessons I have learned because of these experiences. Each experience brought with it many teachings which would go on to reveal the different aspects of who I am, what I believe and all that makes me whole and complete. It is not until one is ready and totally committed to go on an inner search of the self that the truth of who we are is shown to us.

I have discovered that our lives are a journey of reclaiming and awakening the parts of us that we had forgotten and lost touch with. These parts were never taken from us, nor are they lost. Our experiences throughout our lives will either encourage us to bring them forward or cause us to suppress them. "Out of sight, out of mind."

We are born whole and complete, however that may appear, nothing is out of alignment or missing. All we have are our life experiences to draw on to help us discover the essence of who we are.

As a child, I would often sit back and observe the people around me and watch how they lived their lives and I would wonder if this was all there was to life. Something didn't seem right, but I couldn't name or understand what it was, so for a long while, I simply got on with life. As time went on, I would occasionally think about those childhood

thoughts and wonder if it was material things that were missing, because in my life growing up we didn't have much, so I often thought if we had more, my life would feel complete. Or maybe it was a title of some description, such as lawyer, doctor, a master of something, as I had this perception that, for some reason, people with degrees were better or smarter than me, even when life showed me otherwise. Yet, as I got older and did start to accumulate more material things, I realized that I was no more fulfilled with an abundance of stuff than I was in the past with very little. If anything, I was just more confused and frustrated. I then started to think it was a relationship: the ones I had in the past were just teenage puppy love, I now thought, real love! That would do. Is that what's missing? It has to be having someone to love and have love me back, the kind that leads to marriage: I was so sure of myself, only to have it all fall apart. The stirring within, which was always present, is more like a restlessness that never seems to settle; only at this point it became more persistent and nagging. Somehow my spirit found a glimmer of light under all those layers and called out to wake up and turn within. It didn't happen overnight, as I've shared with you throughout this book. My resistance and fear was immense and there was a lot of kicking and screaming in the process of letting go of things that no longer served a purpose in my life. The struggles were many and, at times, the pain would overwhelm me, but my desire to know the truth about who I was and the purpose of my life was far greater and a driving force to keep going. Life doesn't give us what we want; it gives us what we need. We then choose what we do with it.

I learned that religion and philosophy is not a bad thing, not because we need to worship real or false gods,

In Search of my Soul

but it's about having faith in something greater than us and if the religion or philosophy you choose tells you to look within, or 'The kingdom of God is within' then believe that and turn your attention inside yourself, because everything you need or ever want to know about yourself is in there. Sometimes we need help to discover that. Spirituality is not religion, it is an exploration of yourself, getting to know your spirit not someone else's and your spirit will guide you and reveal you to yourself if you take the time to listen and trust. If your religion supports your spirituality, then that's a good thing and it's good to share with others and have that support as you journey within. If, on the other hand, your religion or philosophy tells you something different, then I strongly advise you to question why you are there and who you are really serving.

My spiritual journey took me to many different religions and philosophies and while I didn't really understand spirituality at the time, many didn't feel right, so I would move on. I did eventually find a path that felt right and taught me a lot, but the greatest gift I got from this path was self-realization. I got to know me, not through the eyes or beliefs of others, but through my own. I have learned to trust my own body, mind and soul. I have learned that love was always present in my life and it was only my distorted perception that prevented me from seeing and feeling it. This inner journey will take you down many rough and rugged roads, covered in rocks, debris and, at times, in the dark, you will be made to climb many mountains. And just when you think you know where you're heading, there is a bend in the road that makes you feel like you are back where you started. I can assure you, once you start this journey, you don't go back to the beginning. You go back to reclaim another aspect of yourself: "Life can only be understood backwards, but it must be lived forward." Each chapter I have shared with you taught me many things about life. These experiences taught me to look beyond the surface and delve a little deeper to gain a greater understanding of life and its meaning. If we allow our experiences and lessons to teach us, we become better mothers, better daughters, friends, lovers, wives, husbands, better human beings, not for the benefit of others, but because we become aligned with the greater part of our spirit that is love. And when we live from this place, we have more compassion, empathy and tolerance for other human beings. Life becomes more fulfilling and enjoyable, even the simplest tasks become enjoyable. When we allow ourselves to become students of life, it reveals its true wonder. I could have chosen to ignore my calling and allow my depressed state to consume me and I could've listened to my doctor, who thought antidepressants were the answer and probably would have led a miserable existence, feeling like a victim of life and learning very little from the experiences that came my way. I didn't want to live as a victim, I didn't want pity, and I wanted to live a fulfilling and purposeful life that had substance. I wanted to live a life that made a difference. I didn't believe that life was so shallow that we just existed, then died and it was all for nothing. Life does have substance, it has essence and it has meaning. It is up to us to discover what that is in our own lives and then show others

In Search of my Soul

the way. I hope that, through opening up my life and sharing with you, the reader that I have given you something to think about in your own life and that I have inspired you to find the substance and meaning in that life, because I can assure you it is there; it always has been, waiting for you to bring it to fruition.

Don't be afraid to take the road less travelled. It takes courage, stamina and perseverance; it takes a brave heart and faith, but you will never travel alone and your efforts will not go unnoticed.

My journey is far from over and writing this book is just the beginning of another mountain that I need to climb.

Only, this time I climb with no hesitation, minimal fear and a heart full of love that wants to share the greatness of spirit with all of you. Don't ever give up on the amazing gift of your life. Don't be afraid to look inside yourself; you are so much more than you think you are and you are capable of so much more than you might believe.

"Wherever you go in your life, go with all your heart."

I wish you peace on your journey.

God bless.

Lucy Pignataro

> *"Our deepest fear is not that we are inadequate.*
> *Our deepest fear is that we are powerful beyond measure.*
> *It is our light, not our darkness that most frightens us.*
> *We ask ourselves, who am I to be?*
> *Brilliant, gorgeous, talented, fabulous?*
> *Actually, who are you not to be?*
> *You are a child of God.*
> *Your playing small does not serve the world.*
> *There is nothing enlightening about shrinking so that other people won't feel insecure around you.*
> *We are all meant to shine, as children do.*
> *We were born to make manifest the glory of God that is within us.*
> *It's not just in some of us; It's in everyone.*
> *And, as we let our own light shine, we unconsciously give other people permission to do the same.*
> *As we are liberated from our own fear, our presence automatically liberates others."*

"Marrianna Williamson"

About the Author

Lucy Pignataro is and always has been both inquisitive and passionate about life and the way we live it. Continually aspiring to look for the best in herself and ours. As a Counselor, Life coach and Reiki therapist that Lucy helps others to find their way and aspire to better ways of living. As a wife and mother she finds joy and fulfillment in sharing her life with the people she loves unconditionally and that are a great source of encouragement and inspiration.

It is Lucy intention that through this sharing of her life experiences and lessons that others are encouraged to bring forth their gifts and wisdom.

God Bless

www.ingramcontent.com/pod-product-compliance
Lightning Source LLC
Chambersburg PA
CBHW032337300426
44109CB00041B/1212